Preface
or
Why I Decided to Write This Book

What you are about to read is a culmination of years of extensive research conducted by myself and a lot of other unwitting people from the highly esteemed School of Hard Knocks. You see, I have been working as a Human Resources practitioner for many years now and have been able to observe first hand, and in many cases, experience myself, a lot of things that have helped careers grow. In the same vein, I have also witnessed things that have caused otherwise promising careers to derail. As I have become older and (a little) wiser, I realized that had someone shared these things with me earlier in my career, I might have fewer battle scars.

Before we go much further, I should probably answer the burning question before you, which is "what exactly is a Human Resources practitioner?" A Human Resources practitioner is someone who works in the field of Human Resources (HR for short). Maybe you have heard this before but a company's most valuable asset (or resource) is their employees (which, in most cases are human) - hence Human Resources. As with most professions, Human Resources is made up of a number of specialties: Recruiting, Benefits, Organizational Development and Training, Payroll, Compensation, and Employee Relations is a good sampling. Though it is certainly not all-inclusive. I have worked in pretty much every facet of Human Resources, though the area I have done the most work in is Employee Relations. This is that part of HR that deals with the relationship between the employees and management (aka the company), which means that I am the guy that you would probably come to if you have a problem with your manager. I am also the guy your manager comes to if they have a problem with you. In this role as counselor and business advisor, I have had the unique opportunity to coach associates who want to grow in their careers, and I have also worked with executives who are responsible for hiring, developing and promoting individuals. Of course, the opposite is true as well. I have also been in the situation where I have had to coach executives on how to effectively manage their employees. I have worked with executives on what characteristics they want to see in their employees, and what they do not. What makes someone eligible for the fast track, if you will, and what holds them back. Sure, if you work hard and know your stuff you will eventually get recognized, but what about the little things? People are human and we all have biases. We can easily make a mountain out of a molehill, which can have lasting consequences on your career. My intent in writing this book is to bring these things to light and help you avoid the bad things and capitalize on the good ones.

I have attempted to arrange this book in some semblance of your career progression. I start out talking about first professional jobs, then progress to the point to where you are managing other employees. My hope is that this will be a resource for you to refer to from time to time. I have a collection of books that move with me from job to job that falls into this category. It would be my honor for this book to have such a place with you.

Just a couple of other housekeeping items before we delve into this. First off, while this is based on actual observations and events, I have made significant changes to the names, occupations, companies, etc. to protect anyone involved. Second, while this book was written with those starting out in their careers in mind, I believe that there is a lot we can all learn here. This book is a culmination of observations throughout my career. If you are a seasoned veteran yourself, you most definitely know that we are little more than an aggregate of our experiences. Finally, this is the first edition of this book, and while it encompasses what I have seen thus far I have no intention of retiring anytime soon. To that end, I would welcome your own observations or experiences that you have learned from. I can't promise anything in return other than my undying gratitude (and a possible mention in future projects). I can be reached at jim@hrforyall.com.

Cheers!

James (Jim) Perkins

Ah, first jobs...

OK, here's a bit of breaking news for the new graduate. Chances are better than slim that you are not going to be the head honcho two years out of college (unless maybe you are going into the family business, or starting your own firm). So, with that out of the way, let's talk about first jobs, post-graduation. I don't care what your degree was in. I don't care how many post-graduate degrees you have or what your rank was when you graduated – your first job in the "real world" is an extension of your education.

When you take your first job, you have the excuse (at least for a while) of this being, well, your first REAL job, so TAKE ADVANTAGE OF IT:

Ask a lot of questions
Don't be afraid to make mistakes
If you see something that doesn't make sense, ask
Don't let hierarchies get in the way
Become a "mentor collector"
Pursue what you are passionate about
And finally, don't be afraid to leave if it isn't what you want, or if you outgrow it

Of course, this also applies if you are not new. I think everyone should do these things, but for some reason, we don't. And by "we", I mean me.

That's not to say that you aren't going to have your share of frustrations – namely everyone is going to treat you like a kid and that you don't know anything, but be patient and learn.

When I graduated from college, I ended up working for a company that I had no long-term aspirations for, so I made a move into an entirely different field – sales. But the story doesn't end there. I made another drastic career change, this time into HR. While it is hard to explain now, I couldn't have made that move had I not worked the other two jobs prior. You don't have to stay at the same company, or the same job forever, but while you are there make certain you are getting more than just a paycheck.

Take this career and shove it

When I graduated from college I set the goal for myself to land a job before I walked across the stage. I was anxious to get out and make my mark, so I sold myself hard in my quest to find work. I reached my goal by being offered a job as a Store Manager for a now-defunct auto parts chain. While it wasn't what I would call my dream job, it was still a lot of fun. I worked with some very talented mechanics and other retail people who knew their way around a motor as well as a plan-o-gram (which is to say they knew how to merchandise better than the computer-generated printouts that we received every few weeks), as well as some extremely talented salespeople. At the end of the day, I knew it wasn't something wanted to do forever and after about a year, I decided I needed to try my hand at something else.

My next gig was working as a Financial Advisor, which was quite a change from selling spark plugs and tires. It was during this brief stint that I met a former Human Resources professional who had retired as a Benefits Manager for a large company with the thought of applying his knowledge in insurance and 401(k)s to the world of financial advice. Nothing against financial services, but I realized pretty early in that this wasn't where I saw myself in 5 years, so I started thinking about what I liked about my last two jobs and what I didn't. I became especially interested in my new co-worker (the former Benefits Manager), so we struck up a conversation. The rest is history I suppose, because that was the impetus for me to seek out a position in HR – hoping to leverage my newly acquired knowledge of financial instruments and insurance to get into an HR Department. I ultimately landed in a small HR Department (I was the third employee), assigned the task of teaching employees about their benefits. It took what I loved about my retail days (interacting with people) and financial planning (selling a product), but without all the stuff I wasn't fond of (the retail hours or the 100% commission pay schedule). I found my niche. I finally knew what I wanted to do with the rest of my life.

Sort of.

OK, so I didn't want to spend the rest of my life teaching people about the tax benefits and financial rewards (thanks to the company's generous match) of participating in the 401(k), still, this was the start of my HR career. Many years later, I am still working in HR and I love every day of it.

OK, at least most days. C'mon, no job is perfect.

The moral of this story is that while there is nothing wrong with managing retail, it just wasn't for me. Fortunately, I realized that and moved on quickly. The same went for financial planning, but now, after many years in HR, I am in a career that I actually love. None of this is to say that I couldn't still make a career change, but it does get more difficult with time.

When I first started working as a Recruiter, it was for a retailer. In the retail world, the one position that is coveted above almost all others is that of Buyer. Essentially this is the person who makes the large purchases of various products that the store carries. Typically, you start out as an Assistant Buyer (or some equivalent position) before moving into a full-fledged Buyer role. When I would post for an Assistant Buyer opening I inevitably received a flood of internal resumes from both Assistant Managers and full-fledged Store Managers looking to make a career change. Many of these candidates were highly qualified; they knew the company, were familiar with the product, were very organized, and most of them had a strong work ethic. If any of these traits were missing, they were usually weeded out in short order. The problem was, in order to make the move from Assistant Manager or Store Manager to Assistant Buyer almost always meant a pay cut; sometimes a substantial one. When you would talk about money, they would start to tell you how they had a family and they had this and they had that. While these were managers who were looking to do something else, the problem was they either waited too long, lived outside of their means, or both. It is a lot easier to make a change when you are a year or two out of college and still acclimating to making little more than minimum wage, than after you have done something for a long time and watched as your income and lifestyle improved.

The other issue you run into if you stay in a position too long is you run the risk of being typecast, like an actor who ends up starring in the same movie genre over and over again. Let me illustrate: I recently returned from a family vacation in Florida where, among other things, we visited Universal Studios. While we were there, we stopped in for a bite of lunch at a place that was centered around old school monsters, namely Dracula, Frankenstein, and the Creature from the Black Lagoon. As I looked around at all the pictures, props and movie posters, I couldn't help but notice the same actors and directors were in virtually all of the movies. Sure, maybe Boris Karloff only wanted to star in monster movies, but what if later in his career he had said: "you know, I don't want to do 'Dracula Returns, and This Time He Means Business,' I want to be in that Western that John Ford is filming." Do you think he would have gotten the part? Probably not. The conversation probably would have gone along the lines of "Yeah, Boris, we love ya man but, you know, you are kind of a monster dude. People see you and they think Dracula. It will be a hard sell, you know? I am going to go with this other guy, John Wayne. If he doesn't work out, I'll look you up next time, k? Ciao baby."

Mark Hamill played Luke Skywalker in the first Star Wars trilogy, yet until he popped up in The Force Awakens I can't think of another movie he starred in other than the voice of the Joker in a few of the animated Batman movies. What about Leonard Nimoy? He's been in other movies, but when you hear his name you think of Mr. Spock. So, what about Harrison Ford and William Shatner? These two went out and right away became involved in other projects. Are they best known for their Star Wars/Trek roles? Sure. (OK, Indiana Jones is a big deal too, but he's still not defined by it.

Most recruiters and hiring managers are going to be suspect of someone looking to make a career move and "start over in something new" after they have done something for several years. You may say that you have always wanted to do X versus Y, but all the interviewer sees is someone who doesn't know what they want to do. Who's to say you won't flake on them as well? It is essentially like being typecast.

When I worked for the aforementioned, now defunct, auto parts retailer, I ran into guys in their late 40's through their 60's who were nothing short of miserable. They had been at the company for a long time, some since high school. In a lot of cases, they had worked there through college then took store management roles when they graduated, and then they got comfortable. The next thing they know 25-30 years have passed and they were stuck doing something that they don't enjoy and they justified the reason for sticking it out because it is all they knew.

The sad reality is, that there is some truth to their concern. The longer you do something, the harder it is to change. If I were to wake up tomorrow morning and decide that I want to go to work in plumbing, I would have a hard time making a go of it. Even if I went up to a good plumber who was looking to hire an apprentice and told them I was willing to work for less than what he would pay anyone else in order to learn their trade, the cards would be stacked against me. Why is that? I mean, I know with a good teacher and enough time and hard work I could learn just about anything and be good at it, right? The fact is there is nothing on my resume that says I would be a good plumber, so why would anyone give me a chance? As we get older, we become less elastic, at least in the eyes of someone who is interviewing us. Am I saying it can't happen? Of course not. All I'm saying is it ain't easy, despite what you have read from a motivational poster or billboard.

So, what's your take away from all this? Harrison Ford is a versatile actor? Bingo, though not what I had in mind. What you need to take away from this is that when you are starting out, choosing what career path NOT to take is as important, dare I say more important, than what path TO take. Remember the immortal words of Confucius: "Find a job you love, and you will never work a day in your life." If the job you are in right now isn't a job you love, you are working too hard.

If you are in a position where you would have to take a major pay-cut, and it is something that will be hard to swallow, find places to trim/cut/slash and make the change. Chances are better than good that you'll catch up quickly and soon surpass where you were if you are in a role you love. If you love your work, you will excel at it, and if you excel at it you will become a very valuable commodity: one that employers will seek out and your existing employer will fight to retain.

Interviewing 101

If you are going to make your way in the real world, you are going to need to know a thing or two about interviewing, both how to conduct them and how to behave when you are on the other side of the desk. I have yet to meet a good manager who does a lot of interviews or a recruiter who, when asked how they got so good at interviewing, handed me a book or sheet of paper and said: "read this, it changed my life." The one die-hard, true-blue rule of good interviewing is simple: practice.

Sorry, no silver bullet secret tip here.

You have to practice. Practice in front of a mirror, practice with a friend or peer. Sit in on as many interviews as you can and watch everything that the interviewer does and think about whether that will work for you. For example, when I took my first recruiting gig, I sat down and pulled together about 20 or so interview questions that I thought were good and set out to find some unwitting candidates to test them on. After a few sessions, I found some people that I thought might be good for whatever position I was trying to fill at the time and sent them over to the hiring manager. He returned them to me unceremoniously with sticky notes on each with explanations ranging from "Experience is not in line with what I am looking for," to "Too Expensive," to simply "NO," (and yes, it was in all caps, and underlined). I was floored. I walked to his office, plopped down in front of him and asked for feedback. Ok, in reality I asked him if he was stoned. These were great candidates that had been thoroughly vetted. He smiled and asked me when my next interview was scheduled. I told him I would have to look at my calendar and get back with him, to which he replied: "send me a meeting invite, and I'll be there." I did, and an amazing thing happened: I learned something. Though I went in with my well-scripted interview questions and an answer grid, he came with a copy of the person's resume, a notepad, and pen. I got the introductions out of the way, then he spent the rest of the time talking this guy up. No pre-planned questions, just a conversation. He asked what drew them to the position and what they knew about the company, but he also asked them if they were enjoying the weather and what they did for hobbies. I was amazed – amazed at how easy this bloke was getting off! Then, as the interview started to wind down I realized two things: 1.) the questions had gotten significantly tougher and, 2.) the candidate was much more relaxed. He had taken his jacket off, for instance, and he was sitting a little more slouched in the chair. He was also smiling naturally, not the forced, nervous smile that I had seen at the beginning of the interview. He had let his guard down. From that point forward, my interview style was forever set.

That is not to say that this is the only way people interview. I used to work for a guy who firmly believed that an interview should never go longer than 30 minutes. He was fond of saying that your mind is made up as soon as you meet the candidate so there is no point in dragging it out. While I couldn't disagree with his interview style more, there is some truth to that. We all know that you cannot undo a first impression, but I believe that business people should be able to separate their gut instincts. Also, whether we are willing to admit it or not, we all have internal biases. The thing is, you can't use them to make hiring decisions.

So why do I feel that a conversational interview style works best? Namely, because it gets people comfortable. The purpose of an interview is to get to know someone. Sure, it is an investment in time, but payroll is most likely going to be your greatest controllable expense, so you want to make the most of it. It is better to spend one, or even two, hours talking with someone only to find that they aren't what you are looking for than to spend 30 minutes, go with your gut and spend 6 months trying to get rid of them. Not to mention explaining to your boss why you went with this person.

Boss: "So, tell me what drew you to this person?"
You: "My gut."
Boss: "Sure, but what else?"
You: "Nope, just my gut."

Let me know how that conversation goes.

So, that is how I interview, and there's not a lot to it. I am not looking so much for technical prowess in the initial interview. I don't know all the ins and outs of what a Design Engineer Class 2 does on a daily basis. I do know what the company's culture is like and whether you would be a good fit. I usually know the manager as well, and I am not going to jeopardize my relationship with them by sending over a bunch of people who are going to irritate them.

Now that we have that out of the way, there is one almost universal truth in a world where there really aren't any universal truths: I, as do virtually all of my recruiting colleagues, like for the applicant to do most of the talking. I know, I just said that my interview style is conversational, and it is to an extent, but let's not forget why we are here – I want to learn more about you. Even though I tell you that this is a two-way street and that I need you to learn as much about my company as I want to learn about you, the truth is I really only want to learn about you. Sorry to disappoint.

How does this apply to you as a job seeker?

When you are practicing, there are two things that you need to keep in mind:

First, you should do 80 percent of the talking. Especially if you are talking to a recruiter. Remember, they do this for a living and they would rather listen than talk. Of course, there is a difference between talking and rambling. It is perfectly OK to ask them to repeat or even rephrase a question. If you find yourself coming up short, ask a question of them. Just never ask "is that what you were looking for?" The interview is essentially your way of selling yourself. You need to show confidence and a question like that will simply tell them that you are just there to pander to them.

Second, have questions for the recruiter after the interview is over. This not only tells them that you have done your homework, it also says that you are interested in the position. Never enter an interview, either in person or over the phone, without a notepad in hand. The first page should have a fair number of questions you have come up with during your research, but don't be afraid to jot questions down as they come to you during the interview as well. When the time comes for questions, make a point to look through your list. I always find it to be a nice compliment when the interviewee makes a comment to the effect that I have answered a lot of the questions already, but I still prefer for them pepper at least one in.

When the interview is done, be sure and ask for a business card. Thank them and say the magic phrase: "Thank you for taking the time to interview me. After meeting with you, I am even more excited about the position." As a former recruiter, and someone who has interviewed more people than I can possibly count, I will tell you that I am still stunned at the sheer number of people who do not do this. An interview is a two-way street. The recruiter has a self-interest in making a good hire. If they bring on a dead fish who is just biding their time the hiring manager will not put as much faith in the recruiter and circumvent them whenever they can. Instead, the recruiter wants to bring on star performers. People who are not only qualified but who are going to come in and hit the ground running; people who are genuinely excited to be there.

After the interview, follow up with a thank you note. E-mail is fine since they will get it right away, but an old-fashioned thank you card is preferable to me. The vast majority of folks who have gone before you have already sent an e-mail and the recruiter's inbox is likely full of them. A paper card stands out. If you can't get a card out immediately, then send the e-mail. Keep in mind that the recruiter has usually made up their mind before you have walked out the door, but the card or e-mail can make a difference. One note on e-mails: send them from a computer or at least a tablet. The formatting on a phone can look different on a screen and give you an air of sloppiness. Don't let that be your last impression.

Last is the follow-up. A lot of people out there will tell you to follow up with a phone call. I, for one, will tell you that you lose about 5-10 points with me if you do call. While this job is probably your number one priority at the moment, there is a pretty good chance that the feeling is not mutual. The phone call does imply that you are interested in the job, that much is true, but it also says that you are pushy. Do you think that the world revolves around you? Are you so arrogant that you think that I have nothing else to do but to talk to you? A phone call, if I answer, takes me away from what I am doing to talk to you. What happens if I hire you? Are you going to drive me nuts with every little detail? The better alternative is e-mail. A well-crafted e-mail not only shows your communication skills but also shows that you value my time.

But that's just me...

Phone interviews and first dates

I recall speaking to a recruiter friend just prior to a phone interview with a prospective employer. While I was excited, I also knew from experience that a phone interview meant very little; even less in this case because there really wasn't a specific position posted. Essentially, this was what many of my colleagues might call a "courtesy interview," meaning it was being conducted as a favor for someone. In fact, the recruiter who I was speaking with knew this (he had set up the interview), but I didn't care. It was a great company and I was looking to make a change.

When we talked my friend gave me some sage advice. He said, "remember, this is just like a first date. Just be yourself." While the interview didn't lead directly to anything (indirectly I gained a great addition to my network), the advice was good and it deserves repeating.

I have interviewed a lot of people for a lot of positions, from minimum wage to C-Suite, and while I can tell you what my preferences are, I can't give you a magic bullet when it comes to interviewing because every recruiter and hiring manager is different. What I can tell you is what my experience has been and offer some general suggestions where you won't go wrong.

To start with, let's go back to my friend's advice: phone interviews are like first dates, meaning we are both trying to get to know each other. In a first date, you want to be yourself, but you also want to be cautious about how much of "yourself" you reveal. It really isn't the right place to let them know that your family has a history of mental illness, or that you have been fighting a toenail fungus for months on end and can't seem to get a handle on it. The same is true for a phone interview. Be yourself. Be personable, connect with the person on the other end, but do so in such a way that you do not reveal too much, like the intimate details about how your last job was filled with office politics. Keep in mind that your questions can be revealing as well. Chances are you wouldn't go on a first date with someone and ask them how often they change out the odor eaters in their shoes. The same logic applies to phone interviews. There is a reason why recruiters love for their candidates to ask questions, it tells us a lot about what is important to you. For example, asking questions about the company's dress code or attendance policies tells us is that you are planning on missing a lot of work and when you do show up, you will likely be dressed like you just rolled out of bed.

Just like being on a first date, you should show interest in the person, and questions in an interview show that you are interested in the company. It is often hard to think up questions on the fly, which is why you should have a notepad close at hand when you are on the call. As they mention things, jot notes. This is doubly important for numbers. If they tell you that their revenues are up 15% for the year, use that when you circle back around: "you tell me that your revenues are up 15% for the year, what do you attribute to that?" It has much more impact than "your revenues are up a lot this year, what do you attribute to that?"

One final thought on phone interviews: get the interviewer's name. Write it on the top of your notepad at the start of the interview. Don't rely on the name you were given when the interview was set up; people call in sick, others fill in. If you have an interview scheduled with David and Jane calls instead, the top of your notepad should have Jane written in big letters. Trust me, I have sat in for other interviewers and been called by the wrong name. Also, repeat it back to them to make sure you got it right. I once heard of a group interview where three managers were speaking with one candidate. The interviewers' names were George, John, and Greg. The interviewee repeatedly referred to them as George, Tom, and Randy. Needless to say, he didn't get the job.

Dale Carnegie, in his book "How to Win Friends and Influence People," said "a person's name is to that person the sweetest and most important sound in any language." So, get their name and use it. Just be sure you get the right names...

Turning the tables on your thinking

If I were forced to only talk to one thing during our time together, it would be this: In order to Make your Way in the Real World, you have to realize that while corporations are lifeless beings, they are run by people and people do not always act rationally. While in theory a company, whether it is a Fortune 100 corporation or a small outfit with 2 employees, is its own entity and therefore should act in a completely rational manner, it is still run by people with feelings, emotions, tics, egos and pet peeves. Its daily decisions are made by people who have spouses, children, boyfriends and girlfriends, step-children, friends, neighbors, and people they play poker with on Thursday night. Essentially, these people may not always make decisions that are rational or even in the best interest of the company. Sure, these people are stewards for the organization that they work for and when they are at work any decisions they make should only be those that will further the organization's goals, but you and I both know that is not always the case.

Regardless of where you are, an employee, or an outsider looking in, always remember that this lifeless corporation is in-fact run by people just like you, so you may have to change your perspective and think like you are on the other side of the table. You have to ask:

- "Why would I hire me?"
- "Why would I go with this product?"
- "Why would I green-light this project?"
- "Why would I give me this raise?"

Think of it as the WIIFM theory. WIIFM (pronounced 'Whiff-em') stands for What's In It For Me. Before you make the proposal put yourself in the other person's shoes and think WIIFM (me being the person you are making the proposal to). In many cases, their best interest aligns with the company's best interest, but don't fool yourself into thinking that they are genuinely concerned about the bottom line to the company. What they are concerned about is getting chewed out by their superior for paying too much for a product. So why does their superior care? The same reason. If you go high enough, you get someone who answers to a board who wants to ensure that the company is profitable and therefore wants to ensure that costs are in line. So, they are genuinely concerned about the health of the company, right? No, they answer to the shareholders whose only concern is that the company is profitable so that they can maximize their return on investment.

That is why it is called WIIFM and not WIIFTC (pronounced Whiff-Tick): What's In It For The Company.

With that in mind before you pitch yourself or your idea, look for ways to couch your proposal in such a way that it appeals to the decision maker. "If you hire me, I will make you look good." While you may want to phrase it a little differently, the truth is that you need to convey this message to the other person. Someone asks you, "tell me about a time when you disagreed with your supervisor, how did you handle that?" The wrong answer in most cases would be "I went to their boss..." Don't agree with me? Flip the table and think how you would feel if you heard that answer. Instead, the better response would be something along the lines of: "I told them why I disagreed and I stated my case as to why. I explained how this could have a negative impact on her if we were to proceed. Unfortunately, she held firm to her belief and it did turn into a problem. The good news is we worked together to get it resolved and it turned out OK in the end." This response shows someone who is working for the boss. Was it the best thing for the company, maybe not; that depends on the size of the issue. Regardless, the interviewer sees someone who is looking out for them, someone who wants their boss to succeed. Someone who knows if their boss succeeds, they succeed and if their boss fails, they fail.

Knocking down the barriers to entry when looking for work
- or -
Navigating the HR black hole

Recently I attended a networking event. I was looking to fill a particular position and since this was a networking group made up of folks who were looking for work, it seemed like a good place to cast my net.

The meeting got underway and it wasn't long before someone mentioned the struggles they were having because of what she referred to as the "HR black hole." She said that she just couldn't understand why she doesn't get a response when she sends in a resume. I sat quietly for a good minute, being a recruiter, or at least someone responsible for recruiting at a job support networking event can feel kind of like a pizza delivery guy at a Weight Watcher's meeting.

After a few moments passed, I finally spoke up. I explained what I did for a living and that I was familiar with the systems they were referring to, and explained the necessity of them. I explained that without them in place, recruiters would spend an inordinate amount of time combing through resumes and would not have any time to actually interview. The original complainant didn't buy it, she couldn't understand why she couldn't just send her resume to someone. Her response to me was, and I quote, "I just don't understand why I have to play that 'silly game.'"

Well, the truth is, that silly game ain't going away. So, to better understand how we got here let's get a brief history lesson in recruiting since the dawn of time, or all least since I got involved.

It was not that long ago that if you were interested in finding work, you picked up the Sunday paper, circled those jobs you wanted, then mailed or your resume. Then came e-mail. Recruiters started creating generic e-mail addresses their e-mail addresses and putting them in the ads because it was easier to keep up with the resumes.

Then came job boards.

I recall the head of my company's Marketing department coming to me and telling me that he posted a job on this new service called "monster.com" and that within an hour he had over 200 resumes. Now, keep in mind that in the snail mail days, that would have been more resumes than you could expect in a month! We hit the jackpot, and the cost was literally less than 10% of what it cost to run a traditional ad!

Fast forward a decade. If you are recruiting with a straight job board and e-mail address, post for a Controller, ask for 15 years of Public Accounting and an MBA from a top business school, I can almost guarantee that you will get some variation of (a.) a high school student looking for part-time work, (b.) a recent college grad with a major in English, and (c.) someone whose longest work history is the 7 months he worked as a barista. Why is this?

(Lack of) Barriers to Entry.

If you paid attention at all in Economics (college or high school) you would have learned about Barriers to Entry. If you didn't pay attention or have since forgotten, here is the Jim'sNotes version: "Barriers to Entry are barriers that make it difficult for another individual or entity to enter into a space." Can't get into your neighbor's house and watch his big screen TV because the door is locked? The locked door is your Barrier to Entry. Want to start a McDonald's franchise, but can't raise the necessary McBucks to do so? The money is your Barrier to Entry.

The purpose of Barriers to Entry is to limit the number of "things" in a space; whether it is cheap/broke neighbors who have a small TV set, or ensuring that all McDonald's maintain a certain level of consistency – the Barrier to Entry helps to keep things manageable.

The same goes for job applicants.

Remember the old days I referred to, where if you were going to apply for a job you had to put a stamp on an envelope and mail it? The cost was small, I think 33 cents at the time, but there was still a cost. If you applied for three jobs, you were out a buck and a few coppers. Then came e-mail. Now, anyone can just as easily attach a resume to one e-mail as a thousand. As these barriers have come down, recruiters have been forced to put up new barriers to help them cope with the onslaught of resumes that are coming their way.

So how do you get past these barriers? By broadening your horizons.

You have no doubt heard that resumes are scanned for keywords that match what the recruiter is looking for. You have also probably heard that if your resume doesn't have these keywords that it doesn't get looked at. This is a very broad, very general statement, but in some cases, it is actually true.

Most applicant tracking systems have key criteria that they look for in resumes and applications, and they do assign a grade to your application; and yes, many recruiters rely heavily on this. In fact, I would venture to say that there are some lazy ones who rely on it exclusively. A few things to keep in mind though: a recruiter is only as good as the people he or she brings in. If the recruiter is not bringing anyone in, or those people they are bringing in are not very good, the recruiter will likely be using their skills on the other side of the desk before long (meaning they will be interviewing for jobs themselves).

If the recruiter works for a large, well-established company that everyone wants to work for, they can get away with letting the system screen their applicants for them. In fact, I would argue that they have to. If the recruiter is getting a couple of thousand applicants for every requisition they put out there – what is called a good applicant pool – their greatest issue isn't finding qualified candidates, their issue is getting to them before someone else does. If the recruiter is with a small, lesser known company they are not going to get nearly as many applications, so they are going to have to look a little deeper into the individual applicants and rely less on what the system generates. Also, frankly they have more time to do it.

So, what does this mean? Only apply to small companies? Not at all. Just don't limit your search to just the large, well-known companies. The last time I found myself in job-seeker mode, I picked up a copy of my local paper, the Houston Chronicle, and there was a list of the top 50 employers in the city. Armed with this information, I proceeded to mail generic cover letters and resumes to the HR departments of each of these companies. As you can guess, nothing happened. And, why should it? The Houston Chronicle is the only newspaper servicing the 4th largest city in the United States. I am not the only job seeker who read that article, and I assure you I am not the only job seeker who sent 50 resumes addressed to the Human Resources departments of those companies. I am willing to bet as soon as that article went out, those companies started getting letters, e-mails and phone calls.

Let's put this another way. I live in a suburb of Houston and despite having plenty of great restaurants to choose from, any time a well-known chain opens people line up out the door. In most cases, you could drive into Houston proper, eat at the exact same restaurant and return home before you are even seated. For example, not that long ago we got an Applebees. I worked with a guy who tried to get in and was told there was a 2½ hour wait.

On a Tuesday.

At an Applebee's.

Don't get me wrong, there is nothing wrong with Applebees, but there is also nothing on their menu worth waiting over 2 hours for (not even their Riblets, and those are pretty tasty). So why did people do it? Because they are familiar with the brand, they know what you are getting. The same can be said for applying for jobs. When Toyota or Google posts a job, they are going to get a good response because they are well known and respected.

Again, I'm not saying avoid looking for work at big, major companies, just remember your competition. Remember that because there are going to be a lot of other people applying for the same job. Pay close attention to your resume, and tailor it to the job description. Look for keywords and phrases in the posting and try to find ways to put those back on your resume word-for-word. Chances are, whoever wrote that job posting also established the keywords that will determine if your resume floats to the top.

Now, while this is a good practice to do for all job postings, it can be time-consuming. If you can't do it for every job you apply for, at least use it on the ones with bigger, more established companies, as well those "dream jobs" that you see. Smaller, more obscure companies are less likely to have as many applicants and therefore will rely less on automated screening. Some might not even have an applicant tracking system at all (gasp).

No one is allergic to money

Let's talk about my favorite movie star: Robert Dinero (get it? Dinero? (Hint: Spanish for money...) OK, moving on.

When I am working with a candidate to determine what their rate of pay will be, the first thing I do is assign them into one of two categories: 1.) those who are looking for a job and 2.) those who are already gainfully employed. This helps me know where my starting point is.

First up, you may be looking for a job because you are miserable, feel stuck in your current role, or maybe you just feel unfulfilled. Maybe you know that there is more out there for you. You could also be looking because you are out of work, or feel like it is only a matter of time before you are forced into the job market. All of these perfectly acceptable reasons for me to be interviewing you, but it can make it dicey when the question of your salary expectations comes up. Most people in this situation dance around this question because they don't want to overshoot and miss the boat, but they also want to be paid equitably, i.e. as much as possible, for the job.

So how do you answer?

As vaguely as possible.

Let me walk you through a typical conversation:

Interviewer: "So, what are your salary expectations?"
You: "It is hard for me to say that just yet. I am really looking for something exciting and I believe that the money will follow."

Usually, that isn't going to cut it. That is why you need to have a range.

Interviewer: "I understand, but I still need a number. We all have a certain dollar figure that we can't go below."
You: "Well, if I have to give a number, I would prefer to stay within X and Y. But that is negotiable, again depending on the job."

I have interviewed people who flat out refused to give me a number and in those instances, I usually passed. No matter what the research says about money not being a major motivator, it is one universal, absolute, understood reality. The job and all the cool projects and neat people and free M&Ms may be a big enticer, but at the end of the day if you have to downgrade your apartment and start buying frozen pizzas at Costco to save a few bucks, the little perks are not going to carry a lot of weight for long.

So always go into a job search with a bottom-line, figure and state it as such. "I was making X at Acme and while I do not necessarily need that amount, I really cannot go below Y without making a lifestyle change." This is especially important if you are currently out of work. If you walk into an interview and say "I was making X at Acme before I was laid off, and now I want an extra 5 grand, the recruiter is going to scratch their head a bit. Not saying you won't get the job, you may be that good, but it isn't going to help. At the same time, going in with a bottom line figure does not necessarily mean you will land there, but it does show that you are flexible. Also, if you are truly that good, chances are they will at least match you out of fear that you will get picked up by someone else.

The second scenario is where you are looking for a new job in order to advance, or just move on to something else. Regardless of the reason, you still have the luxury of a steady income and you aren't in a huge hurry so your options are probably a little different and the recruiter will know that. The general rule of thumb is not to take less than 10% more than what you are making now for a new assignment. I say general rule because there are some factors you should consider. For one, where is the new position located? If you are currently working 10 minutes from your home and the new position will involve an hour commute, 10% is a little light in my eyes. Factor in commute costs and the value of your time. If 10% means you are getting an additional $5,000 a year and you are going to spend an extra $1,500 in gas, that means that you may end up spending almost 2 extra hours in traffic for a net benefit of about 7.5%. Would you still do it? Many people would, but if you are like me and have lived 10 minutes from your office, as well as an hour from your office, you know the value of your time.

Regardless, the first rule still applies. Never go into an interview without a set dollar figure in mind. In these cases, if you have a minimum, I would be hard pressed for it to be less than what you are making now (again, unless you are closer to home, or better hours, or a chance at a completely new career, or you are out of work.

Of course, making a job change isn't the only time that we ask for more money. Often times we approach our bosses and flat out ask. While this can be effective, and often times necessary, it is something that should be done with careful thought. If you are thinking of approaching your boss for a raise, consider a couple of things:

First, never, ever give an ultimatum. I cannot think of a single scenario where threatening to quit if you don't get a raise will help you. Even if have something else lined up, nothing good will come from telling them that if they don't give you so many extra clams that you are going to walk. Ask for the money, if they say no, tender your resignation on the spot. If you are as good as you think you are, the negotiations will start back up again. If not, you know for certain you didn't have a snowball's chance anyway and it is clearly time to move on. The problem with ultimatums is they are one-sided. Give me this, or I walk. It can almost liken itself to blackmail which does little more than putting the decision maker on the defensive.

Second, overshoot. It is always easier to work your way down, but very difficult to move back up. Let's say you just had a baby and after careful calculation, you determine that your budget suddenly has a deficit of 3 grand a year. You talk to your boss, make your case, and they counter with two. Sure, you are better off than when you started, but you didn't hit your goal either. Let's take the same scenario, but now you ask for four thousand. The truth is, the most they can give you may just be two, in which case you are no worse off than before. However, if they decide to give you the full four, put the extra grand into savings.

Now, before you go off and take carte blanche and shoot for the moon, remember that while Gordon Gecko may say that "greed is good" (it's an 80's reference, sorry), it can have a serious impact on your career too if you aren't careful. Remember, at the end of the day we are all expendable. Sure, you have unique talents, but be realistic when attaching a value to those talents, and before you go for the gold be sure that they cannot find someone else that is just as good (or better) for less.

Silence is Golden, but Duct Tape is Silver

"Silence is Golden, but Duct Tape is Silver."

I saw that little gem on the back of a minivan once. While I don't recall who all was in the minivan, I visualized it chock full preschoolers with their repertoire of screams, burps, farts, raspberries, and repeated questions of "daddy, why is that strange man reading out bumper sticker?"

In many cases, interview rooms across the corporate landscape are not all that different from the inside of that minivan as it makes its weekly trek to the soccer field. In other words, sometimes we all just need to shut up.

I have worked with some extremely talented people in my time, but few will measure up in job skill to two Loss Prevention Investigators that I worked with. They were identical twins, hardly discernible in not only appearance but also their skill at getting to the truth. They could make their own mother, who was probably the only person who could tell them apart, confess.

Seriously. They were that good.

I remember observing one of them questioning an employee that they thought might have engaged in theft of company property. The employee they suspected of stealing sat down and the twin just started chatting him up.

"How long have you worked for the company?" "What kind of hobbies are you into?" "Where did you go to school?" "What did you study in school?"

On and on he went. I started to think that there really must be a difference in the twins: one was really good; the other was incompetent and as luck would have it, I got stuck with the incompetent one. Then, with no change in tone or inflection, he asked: "have you stolen anything from the company?" In the moment that followed I gave serious thought to leaving, I mean this was clearly a waste of time. How could he possibly expect this guy to admit to anything? Then the guy said: "yes," followed by a litany of things that he had taken, not only covering the list of known stolen items, but also a few extras.

I was stunned.

When it was over I complimented the twin, and asked him what his secret was. He just shrugged and said he had "the gift of gab." He said that the key is to just get them talking and let them get comfortable and that is when their guard comes down.

As I mentioned in an earlier chapter, I have been using the same technique in my interviews for years. Too often interviewers rely on a question bank and grade solely on that. If that is the case, it is to the interviewee's advantage since those types of interviews can be studied and learned. However, if you face someone like me, I am going to want to get and keep, you talking. The more you talk, the more comfortable you get with me and the more I see who you really are. Not that you have anything to hide necessarily, but if you get too comfortable you may find yourself slipping and telling me that while your application says that you were laid off due to downsizing, you were really let go because you couldn't get along with your boss – two red flags here: one, you lied on your application, and two, why did you not get along with your boss?

Whether you are trying to avoid prosecution (if you find yourself across from the twins, just give up, you can't beat them), or are trying to find your next big career break, the bottom line is this: the more you talk, the more likely you are to find yourself saying something that you didn't mean to. Words are a funny thing because once spoken, you really can't get them back.

It's not all about you

When I interview someone for a job, I will typically kick it off by saying that it is a two-way street, meaning that when I am conducting the interview I am not only trying to find out if this person is a good fit for the organization, but also whether this is the right place for them.

If you are considering working for an organization, whether it is a separate division or area within your existing company or an entirely different entity, no one is served if you are not happy. You will burn out, be miserable and likely quit or be replaced. The company will not get the full benefit of your talent and they will eventually be right back where they started.

When I say it is a two-way street, that may imply that it is two lanes with one going east and the other going west, but that is not the case. You see, one side may have 8 lanes and the other may be a feeder road, in which case you may need to adjust your speed accordingly. In other words, the first interview is not the time to ask about how much vacation time you will get, or if you can work a compressed schedule, or if you can telecommute on the days of you have ballet lessons. Asking these types of questions during the initial phases of the interview only portrays you as someone who is only in it for yourself and not someone who is willing to put forth the required effort to help the company succeed.

There is a time to ask these things, usually right after they make you an offer. That is the point where they have made up their minds that you are the one they want, and your leverage is at its peak. If they say no, then reevaluate what is important to you. If what you want is a deal breaker, walk away. On your terms, not theirs.

He (or She) got game

Think of the "greats" in any endeavor, and they are usually exceptional at one activity or skill in particular. I was in a meeting once with a Safety consultant and the company's CFO. The CFO prided himself on his seemingly endless knowledge of basketball trivia from the 1960s, something that he proved by testing the consultant with individual statistics. The consultant was right more often than not, and one thing that caught me was his responses. Things like: "yeah, he was a great rebounder," or "he could sure play defense." Not one of the players came out as being noticeably great at multiple things. Professional basketball players are just that: professionals. And just like any other profession, the coaches place players where they can best utilize their skills. The same is true for pretty much any organization. The "coach" (read: manager) is going to place the players with the best skills in open slots. Jack-of-all-trades are nice starting out, but when it comes time to look for people to take on additional responsibilities, lead teams and take on cool projects, they are going to look for people with demonstrated skills in the area that they are looking to fill.

So, what are you doing to hone a particular skill? What are you best at? What do you want to be known for? What do you want to do? Seek it out and go after it. Learn it and live it. Just remember: not everyone can be a great rebounder. If that is what you want to do but just can't get a grasp on it, consider other options. Choose something that you enjoy doing, as well as something you can be great at. That is how you become indispensable.

So how do you get there? If you have a LinkedIn profile, look at your endorsements. Is there one particular area that stands out? For example, I have some experience with Payroll and my LinkedIn profile shows some endorsements for it, but I am far from an expert, which is evident when compared to my overall endorsements. The vast majority of my endorsements are in the Employee Relations field, which is what I would call my area of expertise.

Oh, and if you don't have a LinkedIn profile – go get one now. Just remember, it is not Facebook so don't treat it that way.

Don't be a fool when it comes to your tools

My dad can fix anything, and by anything, I mean anything. Most of his professional life has involved fixing things. From cars to boats to fuel terminals to motel air conditioners, he has made a very admirable career of fixing things that most people simply can't. Because of this, he has amassed quite a collection of tools, from the obvious hammers, wrenches, and screwdrivers to things that I never knew existed, and no matter how obscure the tool, he can tell you not only what it is for, but what prompted him to come by it in the first place. But when it comes to tools, especially those he used on a regular basis, Dad was a brand man. From Snap-On ratchets to Klein screwdrivers, he was particular about the brands he used. As I got older and I needed to acquire tools of my own, I usually balked at the cost of these brands and often opted for the lesser expensive options, though I could definitely tell the difference between my discount-store ratchet and Dad's. Mind you, no more than I used them, it didn't matter that much to me, however, if I spent a good portion of my day turning a ratchet or holding a screwdriver, I would likely opt for the better quality (and far more expensive) product.

While I do not earn my living turning bolts or tightening screws or whatever else, I am still no different from my dad in that I too have tools that help me be more efficient. A big one for me is pens. I abhor cheap ballpoint pens. I spend too much time taking notes, making corrections, or just jotting things down, to do it with a crummy pen. Note, I said I hate cheap ballpoint pens, not ballpoints in general. In fact, my pen of choice happens to be a ballpoint pen. But HR people aren't the only ones. The next time you go to a restaurant take note of the pen that the waitperson is using to take your order, and the pen that they give you to sign your credit card slip. Chances are it will not be the pen that they took your order with. Pens are an essential tool for people in this line of work and they are choosy about the ones that they use and are not willing to let the customer accidentally walk off with it.

If you travel much you are also going to want to make the investment in good luggage. The next time you take a trip, take a moment to observe the people who appear to travel frequently (you can usually spot them in the elite status line). Observe the type of carry-on that they have, as well as the briefcases. I won't give you any brand names, you will quickly see a pattern.

A few other things I have found to be worth the investment: vinyl folders (for regularly accessed documents), label maker and Bluetooth keyboard. Many of these things your company may provide, though in a cheaper version. Some they may not provide at all. Just because something is provided to you doesn't mean you should discount getting your own anyway.

I once had an employee who actually sat on a giant rubber ball she had brought from home because she said that it was good for her back and she found it to be more comfortable. She did great work, so who am I to question her? Obviously check with your boss first and get permission before changing out your desk furniture, but the bottom line (no pun intended) is that these are all tools and sometimes you have to spend a little bit of your own money. If it will improve the quality and increase the quantity of your work, it may be a wise investment.

If you don't stand for something, you'll fall for anything

I am fairly certain that when you are at work, you aren't just sitting there twiddling your thumbs. If you are, you should put your time to better use and start surfing the internet... namely to look for a new job. I know that is not the case with you gentle reader, because you have stuff to do. You probably have a lot of stuff to do. In fact, if you are like me you have a **whole lot of stuff to do**, but how do you determine what you need to be doing right now (aside from reading this book). Do you go after the thing that someone just called you and asked for, or do you go after the thing that will make the biggest impact on your career? If you are scratching your head at this one, you need to consider my original suggestion and start surfing the internet for your next job.

OK, that was harsh. Let me put it another way. Say you work in Purchasing and you have recently noticed what appears to be a redundancy that may be causing your company to be overcharged. The only way to be sure is to do a line-by-line audit, which will likely take several hours, if not days. On the other hand, you have someone from Marketing calling who wants to know if you can get her a different brand of paper clips. What do you do? It depends. It depends because I haven't laid out what is truly important to you. Of course, saving the company money should be the highest priority and very well may have the greatest impact on your career, but what if the person in Marketing is the Vice President, and you have been jonesing for a job in Marketing since you started 9 months ago. The paper clip search will take all of 10 minutes and will give you a chance to make a positive impression on someone who might have a big impact on your career. In that case, the audit can wait. Now, if that same person is one of 15 same-level folks that has little influence over your career for the foreseeable future and/or you have no desire to work in Marketing, then you might be better served letting them know that you will be happy to help, as soon as you finish your current project.

Like it or not, we are faced with those types of decisions every day. For me, it is work on this book, or watch TV (TV wins out more than I would like to admit) and while it is true that I am not always practicing what I preach, it drives home the point: we all have values, we just need to set them out. The best way to set out our values is with a Purpose Statement.

Like it or not, we are faced with those types of decisions every day. For me, it is work on this book, or watch TV (TV wins out more than I would like to admit) and while it is true that I am not always practicing what I preach, it drives home the point: we all have values, we just need to set them out. The best way to set out our values is with a Purpose Statement.

Your Purpose Statement is essentially your own constitution. It is what you base all other decisions off of. It doesn't have to be lengthy or full of flowery language, but it does need to be honest. In fact, you are really just writing it for yourself, so don't worry what anyone else thinks of it. If you are in it for the money, honey, then write it out as such. It is your Purpose Statement. It is what you should be aiming for. The first time I went through this exercise I wrote it out as how I wanted people to see me, not as what was necessarily important to me. I shared it with people, I was very proud of it, but I don't know that I ever really followed it as my guide. It sounds funny, but even though I wrote it, it didn't really have my buy-in. It was as though it was forced on me by society, or at least what I thought the world wanted from me. So sometime later I reevaluated and revamped it. It took some time, a lot more time than the first one, but I ended up with something that I truly believed in, something that is my guide and helps me as I move forward. Now, this isn't to say that it is set in stone. If I were to change careers, or retire, or have some other major change in my life, it may no longer be relevant. Just like a constitution, it can be amended, but it should be done so with careful thought and consideration.

So, how do you go about writing a Purpose Statement? The only hard and fast rules are:

1. Be true and honest with yourself, and
2. Don't worry about what anyone else will think.

To make it a little easier, I am including a few tips that I found to be helpful:

1. Think about your goals, both past, and present. Are there any underlying themes? For instance, if you have a goal to run a marathon, to bench press 300, and/or to swim the English Channel, then perhaps being physically fit should be a part of your Purpose Statement. For example, part of your Purpose Statement might read: "I value health and fitness and maintain a solid exercise regimen."
2. Think about what makes you happy. Now if watching TV is top of that list, think through that a little bit more: is it watching TV, or is it leisure time? So instead of "I spend as much time as possible watching TV" you may say "I value my leisure time and ensure that I have time for myself."
3. Remember that this is a Purpose Statement, not a list of goals. Goals are something that you reach and then make new ones. The Purpose Statement shouldn't change much from year-to-year.

Once the Purpose Statement is written, it is pretty useless unless you go back and reference it regularly. For me, I have a weekly reminder in my tickler file (we'll talk more about those later) to review my Purpose Statement. Though I typically review it more frequently than that, it helps to ensure that I at least look at it weekly.

When it is all said and done, your Purpose Statement is just that – **your** Purpose Statement. If you follow it, it will mold you, so when you are writing it be sure that what it is describing is the person <u>you</u> want to be.

The best laid plans...

Hopefully, you have a plan.

Scratch that...

What I meant to say was: Hopefully you have a *well thought out plan.*

Perhaps you are working on a major project, reorganizing your workspace, or looking for a new job. Whatever you are doing, you need a good, well thought out plan. Unfortunately, the problem with plans is that they change. You plan from Point A to Point Z and everything in between, only to have something happen that throws it off. Someone reminds you of something you didn't think of, or another competing priority enters the fray.

Maybe you just changed your mind. For example, my plan for today was to get up, write a couple of chapters on this book, have lunch with my wife, and meet with a client this afternoon. As I write this, I just got off the phone with the client and he needs to reschedule for tomorrow. Thinking through my original plan, the morning is still looking good. It looks like I will get a few chapters down, I am still on for lunch with my wife, but this afternoon is looking a lot different. Instead of meeting with the potential client, now I am going to spend the afternoon reviewing and tweaking my approach for the meeting tomorrow. If the meeting tomorrow gets moved I will adjust accordingly.

The point is, I had a plan. Was it a complex one that involved a super committee and a lot of PowerPoint slides? Not unless you count lunch with my wife, but even then, there were no PowerPoints. So, when you are planning your day, always start with a clear roadmap of what you are going to do, while also remembering that it is liable to change as well... and plan accordingly.

So, what does a daily plan look like? For everyone it is different. I have a morning ritual that, among other things involves a quick scan of my to-do lists and my calendar. I look at everything I need to do, then look at my time commitments and choose the one thing that will bring the most value to me, my career, and my goals and then block out a chunk of time to work on it. Not a lot of time, maybe 30 minutes to an hour, depending on what my schedule looks like. What I do not do is completely fill my calendar with stuff. You have to have buffers in place, or things will come up and you will find yourself sacrificing one or more of these important things for something that is less important. We'll talk more about this in a later chapter.

Hey! That ticklers!

Every once in a while, an idea or tip comes along that is so simple and yet so powerful, that you wonder why everyone doesn't do it. The tickler file falls in this camp for me.

I first learned about tickler files when I worked in sales. Back then it was nothing more than a large 3x5 card box with individual dividers denoting the month combined with numbered tabs 1-31 for the days and a whole lot of 3x5 index cards filled with the names and pertinent information about prospective clients. When I would call, if they weren't able to talk, or I got voicemail, or whatever, I would simply make a note on the card and move it up to another day.

When I moved from sales into other areas, I didn't see my tickler file as being something that was useful any longer and it was subsequently forgotten, until I read David Allen's "Getting Things Done." One of the major tools he encourages is the use of a tickler file but his was a little different. First, instead of 3x5 cards, you use regular file folders, Second, instead of just keeping track of contacts (though that is certainly one use) you keep track of forms, articles, birthday cards, anything that will fit in the folder and needs to be dealt with on a particular day.

Like anything else, to be successful you have to stick with it, and in the case of a tickler file, sticking with it means looking at it EVERY DAY. If you are going to be away for a couple of days (like a weekend), you need to look ahead at those days you are going to be out. If you are out unexpectedly (or forgot to look ahead the previous Friday), you have to look at the previous days. There is no way around it, it simply doesn't work if you don't keep up with it.

Alright, so how do you set up a tickler file? Assuming that you have your folders labeled, find a filing cabinet that is as close as possible to where you start your day. For most people, this is going to be in close proximity to your computer. Also, based on my experience I would devote an entire drawer to your tickler if at all possible.

Starting with the folder that corresponds to today's date put the folders in descending order 1 to 31, or the last day of the month. For example, if you are in February stop at 28 (29 if you are in a leap year). Hold on to your remaining numbered folders and set them aside for a moment, we'll deal with them in a second. Now, beginning with the folder that denotes next month, place each folder behind the previous month, through December, then begin again for January and continue. Now, take the remaining numbered folders and move them directly behind the first folder for the next month, again in descending order. If you have a 29, 30, and/or 31 but no days to assign them to, I still keep those in order, but slip a paperclip over them, that way something doesn't inadvertently go into them and get lost for a month or two. For example, I am writing this on April 25th, so when I opened my tickler file drawer first thing this morning, the first file I saw was 25, followed by 26, 27, 28 through 31 (though 31 is paper clipped since April has 30 days). Then I have my May folder, followed by file folders 1-24, then there's June, July, all the way through to December, which is followed by January through March. Can you visualize it?

So, how does this all benefit you? Well, let's say you are having your weekly meeting with your boss and as part of the discussion, she hands you a bill for some printing that was recently done. "This needs to be paid, but we need to wait until next month, otherwise we will be over budget for this month." You nod and look at your calendar. The end of the month is in 8 days. The bill is due in 26, which means you need to get it into Accounts Payable on the first business day of the next month. You make a note and move forward with your meeting. When you are back at your desk, you review your notes from the meeting and see the note about the bill, so you open your tickler file, go to the folder for the first and drop the bill in there. Fast forward 8 days: you sit down at your desk, turn on your computer, get your morning beverage of choice and pull out your tickler file and there is the bill with a sticky note telling you what to do. Boom. Done. Happy boss and less stress for you.

Of files and men

If there is one thing that I wish I had known when I started my career, it would have been the importance of a good filing system. A good filing system is so much more than just alphabetized files; it is a well-thought-out system that keeps up with all your documents. On its face, it might sound pretty easy: make a bunch of files and drop stuff in said files, but that is far from the truth. In fact, while most people see filing as a place to get stuff out of the way, they are not only missing out on a great organizing opportunity; they are also causing themselves unnecessary headaches.

Most people see files and file cabinets as simply places to put stuff so you can get it off of your desk, and this is actually good, you need to keep your head clear and not cluttered with unnecessary stuff. That is unless you forget where you put your stuff.

When done properly, a good filing system will not only keep unnecessary paper off of your desk, which in itself will help you be more productive, it will also allow for easy access to the stuff that you need when you need it.

So, think about it like this: are your files a place where you put things for future reference, projects, and frequently accessed documents (like your tickler), or are they a place where papers go to die?

Be honest.

Let's put it another way: your boss walks into your office and asks for something. Will she be more impressed if you: (a.) go straight to the document, or (b.) spend the next 30 minutes pulling out file after file repeating "it's in here somewhere, I know it is."

When it comes to filing, everyone is different and what works for me may not work for you. However, there are a few universal truths that I would be remiss if I didn't share.

First, use a label maker. If your organization won't provide you with one, buy one yourself. Also, always keep a spare roll of printer tape handy. I can't explain it, but when I made the switch and started doing this my files were neater, more organized, and I was more willing to use them and keep them up. I guess it is one of those weird, natural law kind of things, but it really works.

Second, plan out your storage space. When you are laying out your workspace take the file drawer that is closest and easiest for you to access, take a Post-it and make this Drawer A. Then take the second most convenient drawer, and label it Drawer B, and so on. The next thing you are going to want to do is set up your tickler file. I strongly recommend that this be Drawer A, or very near to it. If you are not checking that file every-single-day that you are at work and moving it forward, you are setting yourself up for trouble. If you are not utilizing a tickler file at all, you are leaving a great tool completely unchecked. Once the tickler is set up, move those files that you look at regularly, like project folders, into the next available file drawer. Next in line is your reference files, and finally your archives.

Last, but not least, perform routine maintenance. For instance, if you have a file in your project drawer, say for a project you were working on that is now complete, you need to either archive it or trash/recycle/shred it. Additionally, when it comes to archives, set aside at least one day a year to go through and clean up your files. No one has infinite file space, but if in doubt, I usually keep the file for a minimum of one year. In other words, if I cleared my files in January and something was put there in February, it typically stays. You may be required to retain records for a set period of time, either due to a company retention policy or rules of your profession, and obviously those rules will prevail, but for everything else I have found if more than 12 months have passed and I didn't need it, it's safe to say that I never will. Remember, there is a big difference between hoarding and being organized. Retaining your records is one thing, being able to retrieve them is something else.

Just to reiterate; the filing system is YOURS. When you are setting it up, it must be such that it is easy to use (I would say fun, but let's not get carried away), easy to reference and easy to maintain. Otherwise, it will simply become like a junk drawer where you just toss stuff.

I've got to take a (brain) dump

It is said that we only use 10% of our brain, which I tend to buy into because the other 90% of our brain power is used trying to remember grocery lists, dry cleaning, next steps for projects, what clothes need to be washed, Aunt Sally's upcoming birthday, a reminder to call your mother, a mental note to take the dog to the dog park on Saturday, another mental note to bring extra bags to the dog park, and so on. In fact, if you think about it, our brains are remarkable in that they are able to somehow retain all that stuff. But how many times have you remembered something too late, or not at all? That is why you need to make a habit of writing everything down and organizing it later.

By organizing it later, I mean that you regularly go through your notes and decide what you are going to do with it. Is it something you need to act on? If so, when? If it is urgent – address it accordingly. If it is something down the road – Aunt Sally's birthday in 3 weeks, for instance, then your tickler file is a great place to stick a note.

That said, one thing I cannot stress enough is the importance to set aside time once a week to go through all your stuff and pull it all together. That would include your notes. This helps minimize the likelihood that something will get misplaced.

Another critical point here – as tempting as it is, minimize where you keep notes. Personally, I use my cellphone. In addition to my to-do app, I also use the native notes function and voice recorder. These are pretty much my only idea catchers, any more and things will get lost.

Maybe talking or typing into your phone doesn't appeal to you, that is totally cool. I worked with a very successful

CEO once who carried folded up scraps of paper in his pockets and scribbled thoughts and ideas down as they came to him. He then made a. Habit of reviewing all these scraps of paper at the end of the day before going home. The medium for idea capture isn't that important, so long as you are consistent.

Those who work in corner offices don't throw big rocks

In his book The 7 Habits of Highly Effective People, Stephen R. Covey introduced the concept of "Big Rocks" to most of the world. In his example, he tells of a college professor who takes a large jar and pulls out individual bags filled with sand, gravel, small rocks, larger rocks and a pitcher of water. The professor then brings one of the students to the front of the room and asks him to put everything into the empty jar. The student takes the sand and pours it into the jar first. Then he takes the pebbles, then the smaller rocks and when he gets to the bigger rocks he finds that he is out of room. The professor thanks him and empties the jar out and this time does it himself. The difference being that he starts with the big rocks first, then smaller rocks, followed by pebbles, then sand. He has to shake it a little, but the smaller rocks, pebbles and sand get sifted into the crevices left by the larger rocks. He then takes the water and slowly pours it in.

The story is meant to analogize our time and our priorities. The jar represents time and just like the space in the jar, it is finite – we only have so much time in a day to do what we want, and need, to do.

The big rocks represent what is important to us. What is important to our careers, to our personal lives, etc. The smaller rocks are important too, but not as important as the big rocks. The sand is stuff that needs to be done as well, but isn't as important as the rocks or even the pebbles. The water is what is least important. The point of the exercise is to point out that if you are going to accomplish the important things, you need to schedule those things first. If you are assigned a big project with several major tasks, don't plan to take care of those tasks as you get time. Schedule time to work on it. This is not to say that you want to schedule every single hour of the day, that is counterproductive and doesn't give you time to handle those things that inevitably are going to come up. For example, you can't schedule in time to put out a fire that comes up that your boss needs you to deal with.

Financial Planners have a phrase that they refer to as "paying yourself first," which is simply a fancy way of saying to save money. The way the concept works is that when you get paid every week, two weeks, month, whatever, you set aside money for your electric bill, your cable bill, rent, food, so on and so forth, as well as money for yourself. You have to treat that savings just the same as you would treat the water bill, you make that payment. In fact, you treat that payment with the same level of importance as something like your rent, or electricity, or water. You pay those things before you go and buy tickets to a concert, or book a hotel for vacation.

The same goes for time. Other people are going to need your time, and they will get on your calendar. If you don't schedule time with yourself, you will find you don't have time to do what is important to you. The key to making this work though is that you have to honor that time just as you would any other meeting, and if someone asks you if you have time at 10:00 on Tuesday, when you look at your calendar and see that you are working on a proposal at that time let them know that you are booked but have time at 11:00 or 1:00. If you had a meeting scheduled with the CEO, you wouldn't reschedule because someone else needs your help on a project, would you? So why would you reschedule with yourself? You are CEO of your career, after all.

Elephants in the freezer

Question: How do you eat an elephant?

Answer: One bite at a time.

This is true, with one caveat: when you are eating an elephant, unless you have a big appetite, you are going to need to bust out the plastic baggies and start putting the leftovers in the freezer. Otherwise, that partially eaten elephant is going to go bad, start to stink, and will definitely mess you up if you force yourself to eat the rest of it later.

The same is true for projects. Tackling a big project is like eating an elephant, you have to knock it out in bite sized chunks. The thing is, you typically can't do it all in one sitting so you have to bag some of it and come back later. But like leftovers, projects do not have an infinite shelf life, so when you bag the leftovers you need to assign dates as to when they need to be eaten by. In the case of projects, this is laying out a timeline and milestones.

Everyone has their own way of managing projects and I am not going to try to convince you that I am an expert in project management. What I will tell you is that regardless of the methodology you choose, you are going to need to know the project's due date. Once you have that date, you can work your way back from there and break the project out into groups and assign deadlines.

Once all this is done, once the elephant has been bagged and the baggies are in the freezer, you can line the baggies up and determine the order and when each needs to be done. Remember to give yourself reasonable deadlines, bake in a little cushion on top of that and then put it on your calendar. I say a little cushion because while it is fresh on your mind right now, these types of things can sneak up on you and other things are going to happen at the time as well.

For example, let's say that you need to write a project manual. Your first step is maybe to determine what all you need to cover, which let's say is 10 different topics. The manual needs to be completed in 3 months, which for purposes of this example is completely doable. You decide that you are going to break it up where each task is a different topic and you set your milestones at 1 topic per week. That leaves you with about 3 weeks left over. There's your cushion, right? Not necessarily. Are you going to go to print with your first draft? Are you going to hand it over to your boss without giving it a second look? I hope not. So, you need to put in some time to review, say another week. Now you have two-weeks' worth of cushion. That may seem excessive, and if writing this policy manual is all that you currently have to do and will have to do over the next 3 months, then it probably is. But chances are other stuff is going to come up between now and the due date for the project. People are going to call and want stuff. An opening for a 2-day seminar might come up that you really want to go to. Your boss may walk in and ask for your help on another, more critical, project. Maybe the two-week buffer isn't so excessive after all. Of course, you can always submit it a little early, I am sure no one will fault you for that.

Alright, so you've determined your timeline and baked in some buffers, the next step is to put the deadline on your calendar or in some other system. You are also going to plug in a reminder as well. This is critical and needs to be done right away. Do it while it is fresh on your mind, while you are caught up in the moment of the project. Caught up in the excitement. Otherwise, you will drift off to other things and this will be something you remember only once you are well behind schedule.

Dear Diary

Some time ago, a company I was working at had a very talented executive who left the organization rather abruptly. While moving into the office vacated by his predecessor, his replacement stumbled onto a journal that was tucked into one of the desk drawers. I recall getting the journal and looking through it and instantly realizing that this was more than just a recording of the day's events, it was a true reflection of what he had seen. He made very honest assessments about himself and his team (including the individual who would be his replacement). He didn't mince words and spelled out his own feelings for many of the people who were on his team.

I recall reading it and thinking to myself: "what kind of guy keeps a diary?"

In retrospect: a smart one.

At first blush, you are probably thinking that you have enough to do without adding keeping a journal to your daily list of things to do. But before you write it off (no pun intended), consider some of the benefits I have found with journaling over the years:

It provides an avenue for self-reflection.

I do my journaling at the end of the day and I write out what went well and what didn't. There is just something about actually writing that gives insight into how I might have prevented the mistakes of the day, as well as how I can expand upon the successes in the future.

It is a good stress reducer.

There is something remarkably powerful about spilling your guts to an unfeeling computer monitor or sheet of paper. Because it is private (unless you leave it out, or in a desk and have to leave abruptly, as the aforementioned manager), you are free to be brutally honest, not just with regards to what you think about what all is going on around you, but also with regards to yourself.

It provides a record.

My mother used to always say that "there is no greater memory than a sharp pencil and a piece of paper." My journals have saved me more than once with things that would have long been forgotten had I not written them down.

It helps with your goals.

By journaling every day, you are holding yourself accountable, especially if you are writing about your goals and your progress towards attaining them. If you are doing it right, you are being brutally honest with yourself.

So, we've established some benefits, now let me give you a couple of tips regarding journaling.

First off, keep it in a safe place. When you think of a diary or journal, you may think of one of those with the lock on the side. If so, you get the idea. If you are going to do it properly, you need to be able to trust your journal with your deepest secrets, many of which you probably do not want to get out (like what you really think about your boss and his management style).

The second thing to remember with a journal is that it is for you, and you alone. No one needs to know that you keep one. I cannot think of a single good reason to tell people that you are keeping a journal (unless, of course you are writing a book about success tips and one of those tips is to keep a journal). That being said, you need to be selective when you write in it and you need to be careful what it looks like. If you decide to keep it in a separate notebook, don't write "Susan's Journal – PRIVATE" on the outside. Trust me on this, you are just asking for trouble. At the same time, I would forgo the fancy leather binder as well, because all that is good for is drawing attention to what you are doing. Visualize someone coming over your cube and the see a 5X8 book with lined pages and a sewn in ribbon page marker open on your desk. The odds are better than good that they will point blank ask "are you writing in a journal?" If you do keep a handwritten journal, use a regular spiral or composition notebook and keep it in a locked drawer. If you keep it electronically on your PC, encrypt it with a password.

Regarding the medium, I don't think that really matters. I have heard it said that you are freer to write with a notebook and pen or pencil, but I don't think that matters. I am a digital guy myself, but that is probably because so much of my job consists of paper in some form or fashion, any chance I get to cut down on the amount of paper I have, I am going to take advantage of it. When you do decide on a medium, stick with it.

The big picture show

The "Real World" is full of phrases that most of the people who say them really don't know what they mean. One of these gems is "Thinking Big Picture," which if you think about it is pretty self-explanatory. If you go and look at a painting or photograph, you tend to step back and take the whole thing in. You don't typically get right up on it and make your entire assessment based on a small piece of the painting or at least not at first.

The same goes for "Thinking Big Picture," everything you do should directly correlate to something bigger than the individual task you are working on at that moment. If not, why are you working on it?

Another way to look at Big Picture Thinking is to look at things as projects. Have you ever sat in on a project of some sort or another? It could be a team project you worked on in school, or maybe it was a big initiative you rolled out in your professional career. Whatever the case, I am fairly certain you and the other team members had some idea of what you were trying to accomplish (if not, I would venture to guess that your project didn't go quite as planned).

A lot of resources have been devoted to Project Management; as it should be. Major, complex projects need a solid project manager to guide them, otherwise they inevitably fail and result in a huge waste of time and money along the way. But the simple fact is, Project Management is nothing more than ensuring the end result, the "Big Picture," if you will, is accomplished on time and on budget.

So why don't we apply those same principles to our daily work? Think about what you are working on right now.

What is the planned end result? Is it going to make things easier for you in the long run? Is it going to bring you closer to your goals? If not, why are you doing it? If the answer is because your boss told you to do it, then I am going to venture a guess that continuing to be employed and/or in good standing with your company is critical to achieving some of your goals, so that is a valid reason. If the answer is because it is easy, you should probably stop.

Now take a look at your to-do list: is it a step-by-step guide to getting things that *matter* done? Your to-do list defines your work, your to-do list is your blueprint to success. Does this mean that your to-do list doesn't include some one-off stuff? Sure it does. It has to, or else you'd forget (don't fool yourself, you'd forget something), but it is much more than that:

Let's say you are tasked with executing a new brand strategy for your company, not something that you write on your to-do list and check off at the end of the day:

    __ Call Tom about lunch

    __ Forward report on Customer Satisfaction to Susan

    __ Develop and successfully execute brand strategy for entire organization

If only it were that easy. You are going to give this some serious thought. There are going to be a lot of components, such as:

- Who are the stakeholders?
- Who can you partner with on this initiative?
- What is your timeline? How often do you need to follow up?

- How do you conduct research?
- What is your budget?
- Is there anyone else on this team, or is it just you?
- What is the priority in terms of other projects in the company?
- (etc., etc., etc.)

Then you determine your next step, and that next step is...

(Are you ready for this?)

A task. As in a task that goes on your to-do list.

So, back to our brand strategy project. Let's say you are given this project by your boss.

As you work through the project, your steps may look something like this:

1. Assemble team
2. Conduct customer focus groups
3. Analyze data from focus groups
4. Develop proposal and present to leadership
5. Develop new media campaign
6. Educate staff on new strategy
7. Roll out new media campaign
8. Develop new signage
9. Distribute new signage
10. Conduct follow up focus groups to measure success of new program

Of course, this is extremely over simplified, but that doesn't change the fact that pretty much every one of the above points will need to be broken out into smaller tasks. Take "Conduct customer focus groups," for instance. Some tasks that may be involved in this might be:

1. Researching participants

2. Hiring a consultant to conduct the focus groups (or determining who can conduct the focus groups for you)
3. Locating and reserving a location
4. Vetting out the questions to be asked
5. Getting legal approval for the questions
6. Determining what incentives, if any, you are going to offer for someone to be involved in the focus group, and ensuring that you have the money
7. Determining the size of the focus group

That is just off the top of my head, clearly there are going to be a whole lot more, and as you delve into this, other things are going to surface and some will shoot off from these tasks.

The bottom line is this: obviously these are all important tasks, so why aren't they on your to-do list? "Schedule hair appointment" is there. "Follow up with Brooke on being added to Marketing distro e-mail list" is there. "Review Ron's proposal on increasing web traffic" is there…

So, we know to add tasks for big projects because they are important, but think this through a step further: a project is really nothing more than a set of tasks. Applying the same logic allows you to accomplish more and have fewer things drop off. Whether we want to admit it or not, careers are made on the little things just as much as the big ones. If you don't hit it on the little things, you will never get a chance at the big things. Show your organization that you can handle the little things and they will trust you with bigger things. Show them you are capable of handling bigger things and they will give you even bigger things. If you treat anything with more than one task as a project, and track it as such, you will have a lot better success with the so-called little things, and be given opportunities to do bigger stuff a whole lot sooner.

What do I mean when I say "tracking projects?" I mean everything from deciding on resources to setting timelines. The most important part is laying out the steps that you need to do to get the project from start to finish. This is key for one simple reason: it helps you stay on task.

Let's say that I need to create an interview guide for hiring line workers. I can do it one of two ways: put it on my to-do list as just that, or write it on my project list, followed by steps that are needed. If I put it on my to-do list it is right there with such things as: call Kerri about lunch, make hair appointment, follow up with Sam regarding budget proposals. However, unlike these things, which take maybe 5 minutes to complete, writing an interview guide could take 8 hours or more from start to finish. If I look at it instead from a task standpoint and break it up (remember eating the elephant), I might have something like this: generate initial list of questions, run questions past hiring managers within department, get finalized questions approved, get with IT to have interview guides posted on intranet, meet with training department to train on proper use of interview guides, etc. By keeping these on my project list, I can better see what all is involved and how long the project is actually going to take. Remember how I said initially that the interview guides could take 8 hours from start to finish? Unless you are in a job where you can go completely uninterrupted for 8 hours and can set a meeting with anyone in the company at your convenience, you will not be able to finish this project in a day.

"It's 10:00, do you know where your productivity is?"

When I was a kid, the local television stations ran a public service announcement right before going into the news. On the television, a stark white screen with a clock would appear, followed by a stern, authoritative voice: "It's 10 o'clock. Do you know where your children are?" I haven't seen that in a while. Maybe it is a moot point with cellphones and all the other technology we have today, or maybe it is just because I do not watch the 10 o'clock news. Regardless, it got me to thinking about 10 o'clock <u>in the morning</u>.

I am going to venture to guess that most of us start to work around 8:00 AM. Let me rephrase that. I am going to venture to guess that most of us <u>arrive</u> to work around 8:00 AM. When do we actually get to work? As soon as our computers boot up? So 8:05? Maybe 8:10? Or is it more like after our computers boot up and we have gotten a cup of coffee? So, shall we say 8:15? Maybe we toss in a little "how was your weekend/evening talk. That brings us to what, 8:25, 8:30?

How often have you gotten to work at 8, booted up the PC, gotten coffee, made your social round, checked e-mail, listened to voicemail, sorted through your paper mail, watered your plants, and sifted through your inbox only to find that it is 10:00 and you have back-to-back meetings until 3:00. What do you think you will actually get done that day?

The time from 8:00 to 10:00 is critical time. It is typically when everyone else is getting started for their day, so take advantage of this time. Get the important stuff, the "Big Rocks," done then, because let's face it, when you are done with your meetings at 3:00 and you take care of any takeaways you have from them, you are really not going to feel like doing anything of any significance, except maybe catching up on e-mail, memos and voicemail.

Hey! I'm over here!
(Focus on one thing at a time)

Alright, time for a little myth-busting: Multi-tasking doesn't work.

You heard it here first (actually I am just repeating what has been said for some time, but if this is the first you are hearing of it, then that statement is true). Our brains are simply not wired to effectively do more than one task at a time. What we are actually doing is juggling our attention from one thing to the other. This may sound all fine and good, except that every time you switch from one task to the other, your brain actually takes a break and has to catch up. This is lost productivity and prevents you from fully getting into the zone.

If you want to get into the zone, you have to eliminate all other distractions (as best you can). Phone ringing? Ignore it. Email dinging? Close it (better yet, turn off the notifications all together). Clear away as many distractions as you can, and then take the one thing that is most important for you that day and go after it. Don't work on anything else until either:

- A. You have to stop because of another time constraint, like a meeting, or it is time to go home;
- B. Something lands on your desk that is more important than whatever it is you are working on, or;
- C. You either finish it, or you come to a solid milestone.

So essentially, you tighten up your focus on the most important outstanding thing you have to do. You work on whatever is most important at that moment and clear your desk of everything else.

And when you need to move on to something more important, or you are at a stopping point on that particular item, then you take everything that is related to it and put it in one place; it could be a folder, a drawer, whatever, and move on to the next task, again clearing your desk of anything that is not related to that particular task. This part is important because it removes any distractions you might have to delve into other tasks, especially when the one that you are working on starts to get boring or you run into a snag.

Trust me it is not an easy habit to pick up, however, if you take my advice your productivity will increase, as will the quality of your work.

Think about this for a minute: if you are actually focused on one thing, with no distractions, you are going to get through it faster. This is because no matter how small another task might be, we lose precious seconds every time we switch between tasks; not only the physical act of switching programs or opening a different file but also the time it takes our brains to make the transition.

I can hear you now: "but Jim! Maybe I am working on something that is really important, but then my boss comes in and she needs something, like right now. What do I do?"

My answer?

It depends.

First off, your boss is likely critical to your career, at least in the short-run, so you would do well to keep him or her happy. So, keeping your boss happy is important, right? For most of us, the answer is yes. So, with that in mind, if your boss comes to you and needs something ASAP and you feel that it is a lower priority than what you are working on, simply let them know. If you do this properly, more than likely one of two things will happen; either your boss will agree with you and will tell you to carry on, or he will disagree and tell you in not so many words to work on whatever it is that he just gave you. If the second scenario happens, you respond by saying "you got it" and in fact go after it, because at the end of the day, what the boss wants is going to be more important to your career than what you think is important.

Stimming

The last time I checked, the number of individuals who are considered somewhere on the Autism Spectrum is 1 in 68. With numbers like that, there is a good chance that you have had some interaction with someone who has Autism in some form. Thinking about these folks, you have probably also seen them engage in some type of repetitive motion or activity – self-stimulatory behavior, or "stimming" for short. Stimming takes many shapes and forms and can involve any one of the five senses. It can be repetitive hand flapping or watching the same movie (or part of a movie) over and over again. It can be repeatedly snapping one's fingers or rocking back and forth or side-to-side. Whatever form it takes, it is generally a mild, but unproductive, behavior that the individual focuses all, or most, of his or her attention on. I am certainly no expert, but people who know a lot more about this than me have hypothesized that the reason for this is to focus their attention on one thing and drown out all the other noise that the rest of us have been blessed with the ability to filter out.

In other words, their brains are overloaded.

The interesting thing about this is that everyone else (as in people who are not bothered with Autism) does it as well. Have you ever found yourself getting so bogged down on a simple task that you just can't let go, no matter what? Maybe it is drawing out a process map, as opposed to actually doing the project. Maybe it is some "quick filing" you are going to get caught up on, or that desk drawer that is nagging at you...

How familiar is this scenario:

You start out with a project that you need to be working on, but before you can really get started with it, you have to sit down and talk with Ron over in Engineering. The problem is, you really aren't that crazy about Ron. In fact, you think about as highly of Ron as a bucket of warm spit. So, as you are mentally preparing to go and talk to Ron, you suddenly remember that the My Documents folder on your computer is cluttered and there is probably a bunch of files that need to be deleted. It'll only take a second... Three hours later, you are just wrapping up. Your computer folder now has a lot fewer files, but you still need to go see Ron, but it's late. You'll just have to catch Ron in the morning.

Was that a good use of your time?

All you did was fill your mind with idle noise, seeking out a distraction, in order to avoid the actual work of doing what is needed on the project. All you really managed to accomplish was procrastination. When you are reviewed for your performance for the year, is your manager going to give you higher marks for completing your projects on time, for taking initiative, or for having a clean documents folder?

Now I'm not saying that a clean desk, or a well-organized hard drive, or a good process map are not important because they are. Just never forget that they are simply tools to get the important work done. Your desk is a tool, and keeping it neat and organized maximizes its effectiveness. Same for your computer, retaining unneeded files can lead to confusion and make it difficult to find what you are looking for when you need it. A process map can give you a clear view of not only what you are working on, but also a vision of what you would like for it to look like when it is finished. The thing is, all of these things should help you actually accomplish something.

So, if you find yourself doing something that does not ultimately lead you to achieving your goals, and improving your career, you should probably not be doing it.

Make a habit of regularly asking yourself if whatever it is you are currently working on is really the best use of your time. By best use of your time, I mean is it helping you to achieve your goals and/or improving your career. If the answer is no, then stop.

You're the boss, applesauce!

Let me start off by tipping my hat to Judge Judy for the title of this chapter. If there is someone I am looking to piss off, it is by no means her, so I want to be sure and give credit where credit is due. Now, on with the lesson.

A lot of people want to be self-employed; make that, a lot of people want to be their own boss. They all have different reasons for doing this: they want the freedom to do the work that they want to do, they want to be able to work when they want to, they want to increase their own income potential they want to do things exactly their way, etc.

You may not realize it, but are already self-employed. In fact, we all are.

Let me illustrate:

Maybe it is a dream of yours to own your own business someday. Your current career may be a situation where you are hoping to get to that point, to earn enough money to hang out your shingle and do what you really love; maybe it's a restaurant, or a hobby store, or a clothing store, or a consulting firm, or a software outfit, or a bike shop, or a multi-national conglomerate. Whatever the case, just because you aren't there yet doesn't mean that you shouldn't start practicing now. Treat your employer as your customer. Think about the fact that if you want to make more money, get more prestige, a bigger office, cooler title, keys to the washroom, whatever, you need to start showing them that you are worth it. You need to learn and understand what they are looking for in a vendor that is providing the services that you are, and then do them better than any potential competitor. Be good enough that they never feel the need to "go out to bid."

In other words, make yourself indispensable. It may be hard to understand, but unless you work for a non-profit, your employer is looking to maximize their profits, and even if you work for the government or a non-profit, they are still looking to make the most with their limited resources. What all this means is if they feel they aren't getting their money's worth out of you, they will find someone who they think is a better value.

On the flip side, if they think that you are a bargain they are going to look to keep you, even if it means paying more because to replace you would mean either paying more for the same product or service or settling for something inferior. That is your goal, to make everything else inferior to what you can provide.

So, if you are your boss, what do you do for you the employee? Do you invest in the right technology? Do you ensure that your employee has the right training and/or to do the job? Do you give your employee the time to stay current with what matters in the field? What if your employee decides to slack off and surf the internet for half the day? Tweet about his exploits the night before? Come in hung over? You would fix the behavior, probably by showing them the door. If you are the boss, and you find some behaviors that are not conducive to the business that is you, show those behaviors the door.

Give yourself a promotion

I have already made the case that we are all self-employed; we all work for ourselves and we do little more than contract out our skills and services to the highest bidder. So, why not take that concept a step further and actually hang out your own shingle?

Now don't get me wrong. I am not advocating that you drop your main client, aka your employer and pursue your dream, selling off all your possessions along the way to stay afloat. There seems to be this myth that you cannot have your own business while working for someone else, though the truth is that most of the time you can. What I am suggesting is to start a side business, preferably linked to what you do in your day job. Some jobs this is easier than others, I get it. But almost any expertise can be somehow leveraged in a part-time consulting capacity at the minimum for smaller companies who may need someone with your skills for a special project, or simply can't afford to hire someone like you full-time.

Regardless, when you do this, and by *this*, I am referring to starting your own firm, it forces you to think about your brand. If you are a consultant, or independent contractor, or whatever – you are your brand, so:

- How are your selling yourself?

- What is your elevator speech?

- Tell me again why I should spend money (or hire) you?

Another benefit is that it makes you think about your chosen profession. If you aren't good enough at what you do to stand on your own and do it, how can you genuinely expect to get promoted? How can you expect to get hired away by a bigger and better outfit? If you don't have the knowledge, skills, and abilities to step out on your own, you should either:

- Set out to get the knowledge

    - or -

- Change careers, because you ain't gonna make it here.

I hear what you are saying: "That's all fine and good, Jim, but how do I go about starting my own business? I don't know jack about starting a _____ business."

Answer: Start with Google.

You might want to write this down. Google: "How do I start a _____ business."

Chances are pretty high that someone, somewhere has written something on it. In the off chance that no one has tried to venture into this domain, find something that is close to what you do and approach it from that angle. The point is to take an all-in approach to the startup. Print business cards, go to networking meetings, register a domain name and create a website, advertise, register the business name, get bonded if you need to. Just be smart about it. Remember, you are a smart business person, and smart businesses manage their cash-flow. In other words, don't go nuts and then send me nasty letters about how you are living on PB&J sandwiches because you maxed out your credit cards and cleared out your savings to get going.

Now, with all that being said, does this need to be a major source of income for you? No. The point here is not so much to have you start a side business, as it is for you to think about yourself as a true brand, with truly marketable skills. There are few positions anymore that can't be outsourced. Custodial? Check. Marketing? Check. Accounting? Check. Engineering? Check. IT? Check. Manufacturing? Check. HR? (GASP) Check. So, what are you waiting for? Outsource yourself.

Caveat: before you get too far into this, it would be a really, really, REALLY good idea to give your organization's handbook a once over first. There are some companies that have specific rules about "moonlighting," and while you may be able to get away with it for a while, there's a possibility it could rear its head. Aside from moonlighting, if whatever you are planning on doing is a conflict of interest with your current employer, I'd steer clear, or at least talk to your boss, HR, or Legal and get something in writing – a quick email should suffice – to back you up should you need it.

Who's your Daddy, er... Competition?

Take a minute and answer this question: Who is your competition?

If you are like most people you might start off by naming the shop down the street, or maybe the company that you threaten to defect to when things aren't going your way; as in "if I don't get this raise, I will go to ACME, they'll take care of me."

So, I'll ask again: Who is YOUR competition? Not your company's.

Depending on what you do within your organization, your competition is probably others within your own place of business, though not necessarily the people who do the same thing that you do.

Do I have you scratching your head here? Good, because this can be tough to understand.

There is something ingrained in us, I don't know if it is part of our grand design, but we are naturally geared to think of competition as someone or something that is out to beat us. To destroy us. To gain something at our expense. It doesn't matter if it is sports, business, or love, you do not want your competition to win because that means that you have to lose. It is hard to have a win-win scenario when it comes to your competition.

But what is competition, really? In the business world, it is a firm who wants to lure your customers' dollars away from you and your brand and direct those dollars to themselves and their brand instead. Coke wants to lure Pepsi drinkers; Burger King wants to lure McDonalds' customers. So, if you are a brand, then your competition is anyone who may provide a service that you would normally provide. It could be an outside consultant, or a new (and perhaps cheaper) hire to your department.

What if your competition is your customer? Everyone has a choice.

If you are in external sales, or marketing, or anything that is involved in directly bringing the money into the organization, you know who your customers are. The same holds true for your internal customers. If you work in a support function within the company like Accounting, Human Resources, or IT, you have internal customers and they make choices too, which means you have competition. In these cases, your greatest competition is usually the customers themselves because to them the cost (time and hassle) is often less than them just doing it themselves than dealing with you.

Let's say you work in Accounting and your job involves consolidating expense reports for a group within your company. There isn't really any competition here, is there? It's like you have a monopoly. Their receipts have to be consolidated and you are the only one who does it for them. It's your way or the highway, so you don't have to worry about all that namby-pamby customer service stuff, right? I mean so what if you are a little late with their reports, or you don't answer the phone when they call. Who cares if they have trouble disputing a bill, it's really not your job, is it? If you don't do it, you aren't going to get fired. But what if they do take it upon themselves? What if they decide that you are not worth the hassle and they only include you on what they absolutely have to? Fast forward a few months: your boss is looking for someone to promote. She is looking at you and she is looking at your peer (who *does* handle the little things for her customers). When your boss starts talking to those that you support, who is she going to promote?

Who would you promote?

Make it a habit of looking back at the job you are doing and ask yourself "am I really worth the hassle? Am I worth the risk? The time? The hassle? In other words, am I worth the money?" If you were your customer, how would you answer those questions? Be honest. Now, what are you doing to ensure the answer is a big, fat, hairy "yes"?

Market to thyself

It is deceptively simple: if you want others to believe in you, you have to believe in yourself.

That's it. End of lesson. Move on to the next page...

So, if it were that easy, why do we struggle? We struggle because we know deep down we are capable of doing more. We know that we can change our habits and behaviors, improve our areas of weakness and even turn them into areas of strength, but the fact is we are afraid. We are afraid of failing. Afraid we are going to be wrong. Afraid that we are just fooling ourselves. Afraid that we do not have the right connections, the right friends, the right boss or the right training. If we are going to be effective in our career, we have to change our way of thinking. While there are a lot of techniques out there, I will share the two that have helped me.

First is the all-important Purpose Statement. We have already spent a lot of time on the subject, (See If you don't stand for something, you'll fall for anything), so I am not going to belabor the point other than to say that this is just another example of the importance of having one. If self-esteem is something you struggle with, or at least doesn't come naturally to you, it might be a good idea to include something to the effect of, "I am among the best in my field." Or, "I am an expert in IT systems (be careful not to be too specific on this front. A Purpose Statement is a guiding document and not something that should be edited lightly).

Second is your goals. Maybe you have recently changed positions or jobs and you are finding yourself in a new world and you are in desperate need of new skills. A good goal might be: "become the greatest Infinity programmer on the team." Why is this a goal and not a part of the Purpose Statement? Because, while becoming a great Infinity programmer is a noble goal, it is narrow in the grand scheme of things. Unless you have zero aspirations of ever doing anything aside from being an Infinity Programmer, and you believe that Infinity will always be key to your professional growth, I would look to master it, but regularly look to grow and move forward. The Purpose Statement equivalent would be to become one of the most respected IT professionals in the company/industry/field. Again, don't limit yourself!

So, you have crafted your Purpose Statement, and spelled out or your goals. Now you need to make these a part of your subconscious; you need to embed these into your brain. You essentially need to change the way you think about yourself. It really isn't that hard, great marketers do it all the time!

Think of successful marketing campaigns, be it athletic shoes, beer, dishwashing detergent, or cars, the successful ones are the ones that stick with you. For a Purpose Statement to stick with you it needs to be either catchy or frequent (or catchy AND frequent). It needs to be easy to remember and recite (dare I say poetic) and it needs to be in front of you, constantly. You need to review and recite it regularly until it is second nature. Until you *know* it to be true.

Fake it until you make it

By now you have learned the importance of developing and implementing your own brand, as well as ways to make that brand better and stronger. Hopefully, you also understand that how you portray yourself to others is one of the most important things you can do to further your career. If you want to get a particular promotion, others have to believe that you are ready for the promotion. No job is a charity (even if you work for a charity).

But…

- Do you buy into it yourself?
- Do you practice what you preach?
- Do you believe in your mind that you are the all-powerful creator of super-cool _____ (fill in the blank)?
- Do you believe that you are a tough, but fair, manager who holds people accountable, even if you do not have anyone reporting to you... yet?

The old sales adage holds true: You have to believe in what you are selling. Therefore, if you are selling yourself, you have to truly believe in yourself.

I mean REALLY, TRULY, UNEQUIVOCALLY believe in yourself. You have to truly believe that you are a "go-getter who has excellent time management skills and the ability to effectively manage multiple projects… dammit!" because if you don't believe that deep down in your soul, what makes you think that the decision maker you are trying to impress will?

So, what do you do? You remind yourself. No, you TELL yourself.

D-A-I-L-Y.

Go out and buy yourself a notebook and write out how you want to see yourself in a particular area. Repeat 5-10 times, then move on to another area. If, for example, you want to be known as having excellent time management skills, though you really may not think that you do, write "I have excellent time management skills," repeat it 5-10 times a day, every day. Before you know it, you will have fooled yourself into believing it, and the funny thing is, once you have fooled yourself, you will actually find that you actually have excellent (or at least much improved) time management skills.

Don't fish in your own pond

Imagine something with me for a second. You have just started a new job with a new company. You put in the hours, go the extra mile, you are practically living at your desk... Then someone invites you out with your co-workers after work. You pack your bag at five o'clock and zip out the door. You have a couple of drinks and start talking to that cutie from Marketing. You swap phone numbers, a little later you go off and have dinner, catch a movie, and play a round of miniature golf...

So, what's wrong with this picture? Nothing, or at least not yet. Relationships are complicated though, and they don't always end on the best of terms. Sometimes you pick up your bowling bag from her place and stay friends, but other times things can get a little nasty. Nasty as in someone stalking you over your company's e-mail. Nasty as in that same someone spreading rumors about you, or saying unkind things about you. Nasty as in, etc. etc.

Of course, you don't have to break-up for things to get weird. Perhaps your love interest is the jealous type and isn't all that crazy about you getting picked to play host to this summer's intern. Or maybe he has earned a reputation as a player and you are seen as the next notch in his bedpost. Maybe you thought it was casual and he didn't, which is evidenced by him chasing you in the parking lot screaming profanities at you as you go to lunch with another casual interest.

Cupid loves to come to where we work. Chances are you will spend more time at work than anywhere else, so it is only natural that people are going to connect at work, and I am not going to tell you to put your career over love. However, if you do find yourself smitten with someone at work at least take some precautions.

First, prolong the friendship phase a little bit. Take it slow. Assuming that you do decide to move from lunch to dinner, lay down some ground rules from the beginning. Tell your love interest that you usually don't date people you work with, so if you are going to do this you need to get a few things straight.

Second, understand their history. Have they dated others at previous jobs (or more important, at your current place of work?) You are going to want to know if there are any crazy exes crawling around in Accounting. Trust me on this, you don't want to get between an Accountant and their mark, it never ends well.

Finally, look at your company's nepotism policy. If you and your potential squeeze work in the same department, you may end up directly supervising this person. In fact, since you are reading this book, I would say the odds are in your favor. Not only would this be awkward ("I need to discuss your performance and NO I am not talking about last night's lasagna, which REALLY WAS DELICIOUS,") it could very well prevent you from being promoted.

One final note on inner-office relationships, if you do make a love connection at the office and you feel the unfettering desire to drop a quick note of the intimate variety, DON'T. There is nothing that a bored IT Security Analyst loves more than reading "private" e-mails between two star-crossed lovers. Is it unethical? Probably. Is it illegal? Probably not. But neither will make it any less embarrassing for you.

The Three Circles

In his book "Good to Great," Jim Collins advises companies to only pursue activities that fall within what he calls "The Three Circles." They are:

1. What makes you money?
2. What could you be the best in the world at?
3. What lights your fire?

This is great advice for multi-billion dollar, multi-national corporations. It is also great advice for small to mid-sized companies, one-person operations working out of a spare bedroom, someone looking to start their own business, or someone who is looking to grow their career.

First, let's look at "What makes you money." Put another way, what provides you with the highest level of compensation? Now, let me be clear here – compensation is more than just money. It is anything of value that you derive from a job. Maybe you are offered a job with another company that would amount to a 50% pay increase. Fantastic.

Oh, did I mention that it will require you to relocate? Yeah, but we are talking about 25%, that isn't a big deal.

Great, the job is in Notrees, Texas.

Still interested? You might be. Maybe you hate trees. Maybe you hate rain. Maybe you relish the thought of living in a town with approximately 100 people in it. Not everyone will make that move, though.

I worked for years at a company whose home office was in a suburb of Houston. Most people lived in this suburb because of the quality of life it provided: excellent schools, nice homes, low crime, etc. But to live here, most people had to commute into the city every day. Part of my stint at this company involved recruiting and I had my pick when it came to locals. People came to me with outstretched arms pleading to come to work for the company, just so they wouldn't have to drive into the city. In those situations, when it came to salary negotiations, there were hardly any because they just wanted to be close. I had people offer to take less money just to get in with the company. In these cases, the location was part of the compensation. If I got a candidate from somewhere other than the town we were located in, I didn't have the same leverage.

There are other factors as well. Things like PTO, insurance, and "perks" like company cars, discounts, use of the company jet... All of these are things that will have an influence on the "cash" compensation you will take.

So, while money isn't everything, at the same time we don't do this for free either. We get something out of it: maybe it's a check, or cash in a paper sack, or maybe the feeling that comes with doing something good.

The second circle is the question "What could you be the best in the world at?" Let's say you are a pretty decent attorney, and by decent, I mean you make plenty of money and are respected by your peers. That's great and maybe it's the best you can do; but what if you really had a skill for teaching. Perhaps you are the one that is asked to get up and present every time there's a rewrite in the tax law because you keep it engaging and fun (as engaging and fun as a presentation on tax law can be). With that said, are you really in the right field? Sure, it's easy for me to tell you to stop working, go back to school, get a teaching certificate and take a job paying a fraction of what you are currently making, though I have known plenty of people who have done just that. The question is: are you doing what you truly excel at? If not, why are you doing it? It's at least worth thinking about. One final thought: when was the last time you saw someone who was setting the world on fire with their work and it wasn't something that they were good at?

Third, what lights your fire? My dad was a serial entrepreneur when that didn't have the same cool ring that it does today. He was not always self-employed, but when he was working for someone else he was thinking of what kind of business he would start or acquire. I'm here to tell you that my father could have been the most talented engineer that any company could have ever asked for. He would have given them 100 percent and produced at a rate equivalent to 3 other top engineers, but I don't think he would have been happy. Sure, the money would have been great, he would have had greater stability, and he wouldn't have had to work anywhere near as hard as he did, but I don't think he would have been successful, and by successful, I mean happy. My Dad is retired now, and I hope when I stop working for a living that I can look back with the same level of satisfaction on what I have done as he can.

You never have to tell someone how smart, rich, or good-looking you are

Let's just lay something out on the table: I hate bragging. I can't stand it when people come to me and tell me how great they are at their jobs, how indispensable they are, how lucky the company is to have them, blah, blah, blah. If this were true, why do you need to tell me? It should already be obvious to anyone who matters. The same can be said of positions and titles. I really couldn't care less that you are the Senior Assistant Widget Quality Control Director for North America, Central Time Zone. Your value to an organization is not linked to your title. In fact, there is a whole lot to be said for an actual inversion of this. If your company fires their CFO, they will manage. I am not aware of a company going under because they did away with a CFO (unless maybe they were embezzling, or doing something illegal). There is a reason you never hear about executives going on strike. When was the last time you heard about an Accounting department going on strike?

Stop taking out the garbage or cleaning up the store at the end of the day? Customers stop coming, and eventually, the company goes bankrupt. Then even the Senior Assistant Widget Quality Control Director for North America, Central Time Zone finds himself without a job.

It is not necessary to point out how important your position title is. Those with real authority or importance don't have to point it out - be one of those. Do great work, get recognized, and the titles (and money and responsibility) will come. Get hung up on titles and you could end up disappointed when you find that no one cares as much about the title as you do.

To borrow a saying from my wife's grandmother: "you never have to tell someone how smart, rich, or good-looking you are." True that Grandma! True that.

Arrogance: the silent career killer

Remember how your Mama used to tell you that the bigger they are the harder they fall? Well, like everything else your folks told you, this is pretty much a universal truth and something that you should take with you as you navigate your career. In fact, nothing will knock you on your tush faster than a big head. Arrogance will mess you up for a number of reasons.

First, it diminishes your political capital. No one likes an arrogant jerk and let's be honest, there are few guilty pleasures greater than watching said arrogant jerk fall flat on his or her arrogant face. Look at it like this, say that you are the above referenced arrogant jerk, and you find yourself needing a little help somewhere (I know, I know, this is a contradiction – if you are an arrogant jerk, you can't possibly imagine needing anyone else's help, but work with me here). What makes you think that these "little people" that you have looked down on are now going to go out of their way to keep you from crashing? They may do what they have to, but nothing more. Need to stop that e-mail with the damaging memo attached from getting to everyone's inbox? You call IT, and IT will be more than obliged to help, as soon as they take care of the more important issues that are on their plates. Surely no one will read it before tomorrow... You can beg and plead and they will tell you that they are working as fast as they can, but maybe you should have been a little nicer when your PC was acting up.

Another reason that arrogance is so nasty is because it gives you a false sense of security. Too big to fail might have applied to the banking industry back when, but it doesn't apply to egos. I have seen my share of cocky bosses who thought they could do no wrong and then get reckless because they think they are too big to fail. They truly believe that the company can't survive without them, yet, with the possible exception of rogue traders, I have never seen a company fail because of just one person.

I worked for a guy once who was responsible for a major initiative for the company. In fact, the President had named it the number one initiative for the year, and my boss took that and ran with it. Every time he needed something, he would remind the person on the other end that this is the number one initiative for the company, so they could either help get it accomplished or explain to the President why it didn't happen. Of course, it got pushed through and the initiative happened. The problem with this approach was once the year was up, everything else he tried to get accomplished was met with resistance. Sadly, his credibility was lost in the process, and the next year not a single one of his projects was considered a company initiative at all.

You are who you network with

When you were in school, chances are you associated with a certain group of people. Maybe they were hipsters, or athletes. Perhaps you were in the band with them, or maybe you were in a band. You might have hung out with a tough crowd, or members of the chess club (or both, I don't know anything about your school). Regardless, you were probably in some way or another associated with those people. You may not have been an athlete, but if your closest friends were all jocks, you were probably associated with them.

The same holds true now, which is to say that you are your network. If you want to be a Director, become friends with Directors. Not just one, but several, but just as it was difficult to move up the social ladder in high school, it can be a challenge in the real world as well. If a Director seat is your goal, but you are five rungs down the ladder from that slot, then you may need to lower your sights for now and build your social standing.

Now, that said, just because you find some level of success and move up the food chain, don't ignore your friends and pals. As you move up, you're going to need their support more than ever. Ignore them and when the time comes that you need something, you just might find yourself sitting alone in the lunch room with your plastic lunch box while everyone else is eating burritos they bought at the snack bar.

Finally, when I refer to networks, I am not just talking about Social Networks. LinkedIn, Facebook, Twitter, and everything else out there is all fine and good, but it is not a replacement for face-to-face interaction. That is not to say that I am discounting the power of social media, it is a fantastic medium to reach an audience and provide you with exposure and access that you otherwise would not have, just do not allow it to become a substitute for human interaction.

Caring is a competitive advantage

As you go through your career, you are going to find that there are a lot of people whose sole motivation is the dollar bills. Don't get me wrong, I have never met anyone who is allergic to money, but if you look at those folks who do it strictly for the money, they are rarely killer performers. I have never met anyone whose primary motivator was money who was also exceptionally good at their job and ironically, these people are usually NOT exceptionally well paid.

To put it simply, and summarize this book, work is a transaction. We don't do it because we especially want to; we get something out of it. Yes, money is a big portion of that, but it shouldn't be all of it. We should get something else out of it as well: we should do something that we truly care about. If your current career path doesn't fit you, then it is time to dust off your resume. Look at your skill set, your education, your location, look at everything and find out what you need to do to get out of there and into something else. Something you CARE about.

Here's the deal: if you care, you will concern yourself with the little things. You aren't going to send an email without first re-reading it. You aren't going to submit a report without at least giving it a hard look. You are going to put in the hours needed to do it right.

This isn't to say that you aren't going to make mistakes; that your boss isn't going to find something that you missed, or that someone isn't going to take offense to your tone in an e-mail at some point. What it does mean is that you are going to take that to heart and work to ensure it doesn't happen again.

I once worked with a guy who was responsible for the creative process in a manufacturing company. He worked with the various designers, corralled their ideas, and decided what would, and what wouldn't work. Of course, I am oversimplifying his role, but what I will tell you is that he was most definitely indispensable to the company. A company that was growing at over 30% and if you asked the CEO what the secret sauce to the company's success was, this guy's name came up A LOT. Once I was in his office and he had all this stuff spread out across his desk – rocks, brass tubing, copper wiring, nuts and bolts, a piece of leather. As we were talking, I reached out and swept this stuff to the side and said: "let me move some of this junk out of the way." As soon as I said this he responded in a terse and adamant tone. "This isn't junk," he said staring me down. "This is all stuff that goes into our products." He was right, that stuff wasn't junk. It was the core of the company's livelihood and, by extension, his livelihood as well. That is passion, and that can make or break you.

Be a winner by not having to win all the time

When I was growing up, I remember sitting down with a friend in front of the TV flipping channels trying to decide what to watch. We finally settled on a soccer match, though neither one of us really followed, or even cared about, soccer. Regardless, after a little while, we found ourselves cheering on one of the teams. When my friend's mom came in and saw what we were watching, she asked: "who are you rooting for?" We told her and she nodded, before saying, "I didn't know you were fans." "We're not," we replied. "We're cheering for them because they are winning." This is a small example of a real fact: everyone wants to be on, or at least rooting for, the winning team. Like a high school friend of mine who played football lamented: "losing makes for a long bus ride home."

Do you know someone who likes to lose?

Neither do I.

It is in our nature to be competitive, to want to win. Just take a look at opening game day for your area, the flags are lovingly affixed to cars. The jerseys, painted faces, and blow horns all come out. People turn out in droves to root for "their team," waving big foam fingers. We want to win. We want to be number one.

Part of a winning strategy professionally, though is not having to be the winner all the time.

This doesn't mean that you take a fall, or not speak up when you are right. It simply means that you do not make a spectacle out of it. If you are right and someone else is wrong, sometimes it is better to leave it at that.

Maybe you get bragging rights. Maybe you get the internal satisfaction of knowing you were right. But where's the real gain? The person who you just made your point to is now clearly, undoubtedly wrong. They know it without a doubt. Congratulations, but what have you really accomplished? Is being the guy who smashed your coworker by being dead on right any closer to the next promotion or the bigger cubicle, corner office, or position that has greater flexibility, or whatever you are working for? Or are you now the guy that is just a little more difficult to work with? Have you now become the guy who has to be right; who has to win at all costs? Are you now the guy who has lost sight of the business objectives and is instead concerned with winning? Yeah, that is the guy I want to work for. That is the guy I want to fight to keep. That is the guy I want to promote to lead this team.

Of course, with so many things in this book, there is a caveat. Don't walk away and confuse having to win all the time with doing what is right, just remember that there is a right way to do it. If you are right about something, point it out, but don't gloat. Hold your ground if you have to, but once the point is made, move on.

How about a little face time?

We live in the digital age and pretty much everyone spends the majority of their time in front of some type of screen, whether it is a computer, phone, tablet, or all of the above; which incidentally is where the majority of our communication occurs. E-mail, texting, Slack, WhatsApp, and the like are all fantastic tools that have made communication easier and, in most instances, more efficient.

Just don't confuse efficiency with effectiveness.

Time for a little pop quiz – you need to have a somewhat sensitive discussion with a co-worker. Do you: (a) send them an e-mail, (b) pick up the phone, or (c) walk over to their desk? If you chose (c) you win (assuming they are within walking distance). If you chose (b) you are a close second (unless they are not within walking distance, if that is the case you win too). If you chose (a), this chapter is for you (regardless of the walking distance).

Our screens have become a virtual barrier between us and the people we are communicating with, especially if we are having a difficult conversation. Instead of talking to the person face-to-face and running the risk of us seeing them get upset, become defensive, argue with us, and maybe even point out that we were wrong; we prefer to send them an e-mail or a text.

I once met someone who was laid off from his job via videocassette (it was a long time ago). Essentially a videocassette came to his office with a list of people and a memo stating that the video was to be played to only that list of individuals. On the video, the president of the company came on and stated that he was sorry, but the company had made the decision to eliminate their positions. I don't know about you, but I think that is pretty crappy. Message aside though, it is not a lot different than firing off a flamer to someone and telling them how their idea is wrong, or how you think that they are not pulling their weight on the team, or whatever. How is sitting down at your computer and typing up an e-mail that you know is going to rile someone up any different than making a video and then setting it on the person's desk with a sticky note that says "watch me."

Now before you go off and decide that I am a Philistine who hates all things digital and that I am telling all my faithful readers to forgo their use, all I'm saying is that texting, e-mail, and the like are simply tools and like any tools, they have their limits.

Of course, there will be times where an e-mail exchange starts out fine, and then goes south. In these instances, obviously, the same thought process applies:

1. Stop typing
2. Get up and walk over to their desk, or
3. Pick up the phone and give them a call.

It is not always going to be the most comfortable and, by extension, most natural thing to do, but it will make things a lot easier. Just say: "hey, I thought about replying to your e-mail, but thought it best if I just came over (or gave you a call)."

Extra! Extra! Read all about it!

Having worked in Human Resources for as long as I have, it helps to have a rule of thumb or two to help guide decisions. Perhaps one of the greatest ones for me is what I've heard called the New York Times test. This gem goes like this: when you make a decision, imagine that you would read it on the front page of the New York Times. Considering this, would you change anything about that decision? If the answer is no, then you are probably making a good call.

As a professional, you are going to find your decisions being challenged from time-to-time. If this isn't the case, you needn't worry because your job will likely be replaced by a robot in the very near future. Being challenged means that we are thinking. Unlike computers, which operate off of a set of pre-programmed rules and code, we are making decisions that are not exact and are often outside of normal parameters, and the hard truth is, not everyone is going to agree with all your decisions. If this weren't the case, a computer can be programmed to make the decision for you for a lot less than your salary, and it will never call in sick or take excessive coffee breaks. And since everyone is not going to agree with your decisions, you still need to be able to defend them if needed.

So, if someone – be it a peer, your boss, or someone beneath you, comes up to you and asks you something along the lines of "what were you thinking?" You need to be able to answer them with a clear conscience. Does that mean that you are always going to be right? Nope, but at the bare minimum, I hope you at least believe in your decision.

Never underestimate the power of donuts (or fresh baked chocolate chip cookies)

Early in my career, I was tasked with promoting my company's 401(k). It was a very generous plan, but it hadn't been marketed very well. The primary strategy for addressing this issue was to conduct informative meetings with all employees throughout the company.

So, I set out with my presentation, my handouts, everything I needed to have successful meetings, but participation was nothing short of dismal. I had spoken with the managers for each location prior to coming out and felt that they were all behind the initiative. I talked with those who did come and for the most part they indicated that their managers had strongly encouraged everyone to attend, on top of this, I conducted the meetings during regular business hours, and everyone who came was paid for their time. Despite all of this, attendance still wasn't anywhere near where I thought it ought to be. The fact was, they would rather do their daily jobs, which were mostly manual and routine, rather than stop and listen to me.

It was during this participation drought that, as I was pulling into one of our facilities, I spotted a donut shop. I was early so I walked in and bought several dozen plain glazed donuts for the meeting. Wouldn't you know, everyone in the building came. After that, I always found the nearest donut shop and made sure I brought donuts. At the end of the first year of my efforts, participation in the 401(k) had doubled and I received a handwritten note from the CEO thanking me for my efforts. All because I brought donuts (coupled with my fantastic presentation skills, of course).

Around this same time the company was in the process of implementing a new software program. To be sure everyone was acquainted with the new software, the company offered workshops on how to use the software. When I walked in, the first thing I noticed was a plate of homemade chocolate chip cookies sitting in the room. As the software was rolled out, people talked as much about the cookies as the training. Was the training effective? Yes. Was that because of the cookies? No. Had attendance been as good without the cookies? I will let you decide.

The moral of the story is that often times it is the little things that draw people in. Think about what you are looking to accomplish and how to accomplish it. If you need to get people to attend a voluntary meeting, appeal to their need for more than just knowledge; cookies and/or donuts are cheap but can go a long way.

Finding the perfect Administrative Assistant

I once had a Vice President come to me to find an Administrative Assistant, "a good Admin can make or break you," she said, as we worked out the job posting. Having seen both (good and bad Admins) at work, I can tell you that is a very true statement.

But what if you do not have the luxury of your own, dedicated Administrative professional?

This is where Virtual Assistants come into play.

With technology changing as much as it has, the work of an Admin has changed significantly as well, though there are still those "executives" who have not made this leap. For instance, I once worked with a guy who insisted that his Administrative Assistant listen to his voicemails, then come into his office and read them out loud to him. I am not sure where the efficiency was in that.

Don't get me wrong, I am not suggesting that Administrative Assistants are not key positions in organizations, but like pretty much everything else, the role has changed and become more sophisticated. Gone are the days of "Ms. Jones' office. I'm sorry, she is unavailable, may I take a message?" Now it is "Hello, you have reached the office of Deborah Jones. I am sorry I am unable to take your call right now, but if you would like to leave a message, please do so after the tone." That is, of course of your company still utilizes voicemail at all.

If you carry a smartphone with you everywhere like I do, then you have some of the best benefits of a personal assistant right there. Sure, Siri and her kin have a long way to go, but I have used her to draft more than a few quick email responses, to remind me to pick up my dry cleaning when I leave the office, and to read off my calendar as I am walking into the office first thing in the morning. Don't limit yourself to whatever came built into your smartphone, though. There are literally thousands of apps out there geared to make your life easier. Toodledo and Wunderlist are two powerful task managers that will send you text reminders which can be very handy, and the best part is that they are both free. Another tool that I have found to be indispensable is something called IFTTT, which stands for If This, Then That. It is a pretty amazing piece of software that integrates tons of the apps on your phone or tablet to do all kinds of things, from texting you when you arrive at a certain place to turning your thermostat down when you leave the office.

Between the time that I write this and the time you read it, there is a good chance some of these suggestions may not even be available any longer, and instead be replaced with something even better (for instance, Wunderlist was bought by Microsoft, and I understand they are in the process of phasing it out). The bottom line, stop thinking of your phone – company or personal – as simply a way to keep up with social media and stay connected with friends, and instead utilize its power to help you be more productive, get more done, and shine in your career.

ROCK STAR!

I just returned from a trip with my wife to Target, she needed to buy a few things and since I was bored I went along for the ride. While she filled her basket with much-needed essentials, I found myself thumbing through an autobiography of Steven Tyler. As with virtually any book about an aging celebrity who has had fame and fortune dumped in their lap without an instruction manual, I didn't need to spend a great deal of time reading to get the gist of what it was about – outrageous parties and an unbelievable amount of drug and alcohol abuse. There was also a photo section, as expected, smack in the middle - and this was where I found myself whittling away precious moments of my life.

Why?

Because regardless of your opinion of Steven Tyler or Aerosmith, no one can deny that he is (or at least was) the quintessential "Rock star:" Trashing hotel rooms, partying all night with hordes of groupies who worship him, sleeping two hours, getting up and playing for 50,000 screaming fans, and then climbing back on the bus (or chartered jet) and going on to the next city and do it again.

A whole lot of these musicians end up dead from overdose or suicide, while others bounce in and out of rehab, but we are still drawn to them, and why not? Tons of money, adoring fans, carefree lifestyle.

So why don't more people achieve that level of success? It isn't from a lack of trying; there are loads of bands out there, and many of them quite good. What separates the "hey, that local band that is playing at Joe's Pub ain't bad," from the "I tried to get tickets to see this band, but they sold out the stadium in 2 hours," often times boils down to passion; a laser-focused passion for what they do. Focused as in, I don't care about anything else whatsoever but my music, passion. Read or listen to any interview with a successful musician and you quickly learn that they only care about the music.

Do others make it off of sheer talent alone (and being in the right place at the right time?)

Sure, they are called one-hit-wonders.

What about you? Are you a Marketing (Rock)star? An Accounting (Rock)star? Are you solely focused on being the best Copyrighter you can be? The best Staff Accountant? Or are you distracted by wanting to be in the next seat or the seat after that? Are you busy trying to prove why someone else got a promotion you wanted, or are you turning that frustration inward to make yourself better?

Are you worried that someone might call you a "brown-noser?" In the music business, I would venture to say that the equivalent is being called a sellout. Interestingly, I heard someone ask the band Metallica what they thought of being referred to as a sellout. Their response (and I am paraphrasing), was "yeah, we're sellouts. We sellout stadiums every night."

I love that.

So, go forth and be a sellout. Throw everything you have into your chosen craft. Read everything you can find on it. Talk about it with others in similar roles. Go to seminars and networking events. Your career should be your passion. If it isn't, give serious thought to making a change.

Come on over to my place

I don't have to tell you that in all likelihood you are going to spend more time at your workspace than anywhere else, so why let it be sterile? I believe that regardless of what or where your workspace is, you should do everything you can to personalize it. Whether it is family pictures, plants, stickers, movie posters, or whatever, you should make your workspace your own (within reason, of course).

Think about where you live. Did you add any decorations to it? Hang a few pictures? Arrange things a certain way? I am going to venture a guess and say you did because it is your place. The same should be true of your workspace.

A personalized workspace tells others that you have pride in where you work and it tells others that you think of this as more than just a job. I once worked for a guy who had recently moved into a new office. The move took place at a busy point and he never took time out to decorate. It wasn't until his boss came in and asked him if he was planning to actually stick around, that he put up some personal effects. It hadn't occurred to him, but the office didn't look lived in and therefore didn't look like he was willing to make the investment to stay; something that was obviously seen by others, namely his boss.

Of course, there is a caveat. When you are making your work area your own, be careful not to violate any rules, written or otherwise, about office decorum. I used to work for a private design firm that was very particular about maintaining a certain image. This is not to say that I did not have good taste in decorating, but I did have to keep that in mind as I personalized my space – smaller plants and no movie posters; but I still put up personal photos and mementos, toys, and other knick-knacks. In other words, I still made it my own, I just stayed within the company's conscripts.

If you are comfortable at work and feel a sense of ownership, your productivity will go up as well. I do not have any research to back this up other than my own experience, so you are going to have to take my word for it.

Scarcity

Economics has been called the Dismal Science, and it is no wonder when one of its key tenets is the concept of "Scarcity." Chances are you learned about this in high school economics, but if you didn't, I will try and lay it out in layman's terms. Scarcity is just another way of saying that there is a finite amount of dollars chasing an almost infinite amount of goods.

Put another way, here is a mock conversation my high school economics teacher gave whilst lecturing on scarcity:

You: "Do you have some money?"
Your Friend: "I don't have any money."
You: "Why don't you have any money?"
Your Friend: "Because I bought these new shoes."

Now before we all start deriding the current education system in this country, let me just say that this simple example made sense to me, and it stuck.

Obviously, this applies to money, but really it applies to anything we use to barter, whether it is money, eggs, or talent and skills. In the example, my high school teacher gave to me more than a few years ago, if this person hadn't bought the shoes, he would have money to buy something else. If money was in abundant supply he could buy whatever they wanted and still have money left over, but of course that is not the case. No matter how wealthy you are, there is always a limit to what you can buy.

The same goes for skills. If there is an unlimited supply of skills to perform your role, there is little scarcity for your skills. Let's say you are a programmer and, using my

teacher's example from above, the following dialog occurs between your Boss and their Boss:
Boss' Boss: "You need to get rid of a programmer."
Boss: "OK, well, it can't be [insert your name here]."
Boss' Boss: "Why can't it be [insert your name here]?"
Boss: "Because no one else can do what she does." Or: "Because she is better at this, this and this than anyone else on my team."

That is scarcity; scarcity for your particular skill set.
Scarcity is the antithesis of expendable.

So, how does this translate to you?

Looking at your skills inventory, are the skills you currently bring easy to replace? If so, what are you doing to increase the scarcity of what you do? For example, if you are a web programmer:

Are you the best web programmer you can possibly be?
Are you in the top 2% of web programmers If not, is this at least a genuine goal you have written out?
Are you reading Web Programmer Digest? (I just made this up – the idea is to subscribe to your leading periodical and READ it).
Did you join the National Association of Web Programmers (NAWB), as well as their local chapter? (Yep, I made that up too, but you get the idea...)
How many web programmer specific blogs do you subscribe to, and read?
Are you networked with other web programmers through LinkedIn, or some other web programmer specific social network?
Do you have web programmer certifications, even if you had to pay for them yourself?
Do you volunteer for way-out projects that other web programmers aren't interested in? Do you pour your blood

and guts into them as though your very livelihood depended on it?

This isn't intended to be an all-inclusive list, but my hope is to get you thinking: "is there scarcity to what I do, or am I expendable?" In other words, "how easy will it be for the company to replace me, or simply do without me?"

E-mail and the fine art of covering your backside

I once worked with someone who was in the habit of copying herself every time she sent me a note. When she left the company, I was assigned to clear out her e-mail and make sure there wasn't anything outstanding. In doing so the first thing I noticed was an e-mail folder called "CYA" (if you aren't sure what CYA stands for, let's just say it loosely translates to Cover Your Assets). I opened the folder and realized that she had actually created an e-mail rule so that every e-mail where she was the sender and in addition to automatically ccing herself, the email was sent directly to this folder.

That's some serious CYA.

Now, I am not suggesting that you set up a rule that carbon-copies you on every e-mail you send and then plugs it into a separate folder – that is what "Sent" is for, but I do want to visit a little bit about how e-mail is a great tool in your arsenal of covering your ass(ets).

By now I am sure you know the importance of verbal communication and not relying too heavily on e-mail, texting, or other forms of non-verbal communication. While I agree that there are some messages that are best delivered verbally or in person, the problem is that these messages can often be lost in translation later on, sometimes at the convenience of the person who heard the message. Need an example? How many times have you heard someone reply with "that is not what I said!" or, "you misunderstood me." If done properly, e-mail can greatly alleviate this problem.

As with anything involving communication, this has to be done with tact. For instance, I would advise against doing what my co-worker did at the start of this section; I would be lying to you if I said that it didn't annoy me when I would see her name CC'ed on EVERY SINGLE E-MAIL. She mind as well have had "I don't trust you" in her signature line. However, there are going to be times when you need to remind someone of a conversation. In this case a simple line or two to the effect of "Hey Ted, I reviewed my e-mail regarding project XYZ, and below is what I have. Let me know if you have anything different. Give me a call if there are any adjustments we need to make going forward. Thanks as always for your partnership." Now it is in writing, you can go back and find it, in your sent folder, if anything ever comes up. Nothing in that email is aggressive or even implies that you think that Ted isn't going to follow through. If something happens and Ted doesn't come through, and he starts looking for someone to blame, you have something showing that, at least at that moment, the ball was in his court. Hopefully he doesn't have a similar email to you from a later time.

If it's on your screen, it can be seen

I am a privacy fanatic.

There, I said it. It feels kind of good to get that off of my chest. "Hi, my name is Jim and I am a privacy fanatic."

Because I am such a privacy fanatic, I am very careful about what I keep on any type of company-owned device. In fact, you can summarize my opinion this way: if it is of a private or sensitive nature it is not on my work computer or company phone. Why am I so anal about this? Because I know full well that if it shows on my screen, it can be seen. By seen, I mean by the IT department. By IT department, I mean not only the person responsible for information security, but also my boss. By my boss, I mean her boss. By her boss I mean his boss, and so on.

I have worked in Human Resources for a while now, and in my varying capacities I am often the next step in viewing some of the things that people kept on their work computers and the thing that never ceases to amaze me is what people choose to save on their bloody machines. It doesn't matter how many classes I teach or policies I distribute about company-owned electronics and the fact that there is NO right to privacy, people still treat them like their own personal computers that they have at home. A sampling of things I have come across:

- Vacation photos?
- Pictures of their pets?
- The Great American Novel?
- Invoices for their borderline illegal business?
- Near naked pictures of themselves?
- Pornography?

But this doesn't just apply to when we leave a company either. In the world we live in there is one thing you can count on – at some point or another you are going to need to have your computer worked on. Take this a step further and realize that, contrary to their appearance, people who work in IT are people too, and like most people, they range from curious to nosy, so expect them to catch at least a passing glimpse at your files. The question is, are you OK with what they are going to see?

Perhaps you are good about not keeping anything embarrassing on your computer, so you decide not to heed my advice, and you treat your work computer as your personal machine. Never, ever, ever keep any type of personal files on your work computer that you do not have backed up unless you can live without them if something happens. This goes beyond the realm of whether or not you care if anyone sees your files. Maybe it is your family vacation photos or personal contacts. You never know when you may have to leave unexpectedly and you do not want your only copy of your best friend holding her newborn baby to disappear when you leave. This goes for cellphones as well. If you are issued a company cell phone, chances are you are going to keep personal numbers on it. That is fine, but be sure and back these up from time to time. In the event of a layoff or other termination, the second thing that will be told to you after you are told you are being released will be "leave your cellphone here." And most companies do not allow you to sit in a conference room for an hour or so copying down the 200 names and numbers in your phone's address book. There are easy fixes for this, namely automatic cloud backups, but even in this instance be certain that you own the backup and not your company. You don't want to get home, log in to download your contacts only to find that the password was changed by the company administrator.

The bottom line is this: your work computer/cell phone is not your personal computer/cellphone. It belongs to the company. If you remember that and respect the boundary between the two, you should be fine

Facebook the music

The lines between our work world and our personal world have turned into a great big monumental blur. So much so, that most people in HR will tell you that as a rule they do not friend people that they work with.

I understand the sentiment, but personally I do not adhere to this. The only exception being, I do not request them as friends. If they send me a friend request, I will usually accept it.

The truth is, many of my most enduring friendships are from people I either currently work with or have worked with in the past, so I would be lying if I said that I never friend people I work with. But, and this is a BIG but, I am very careful about what I put out there. In fact, I rarely talk about work at all.

We all know that nothing is really secure out there in cyberspace-land. In fact, Facebook and its ilk continues to provide job security for me and my fellow HR practitioners. I have had to deal with some very intelligent people who for whatever reason thought that there was no way that something they said about someone else would ever get past their 1500 friends and followers, so they run their online mouths about the Supplies Buyer who insists on buying the cheap ballpoints that leak all over their desk drawer. Then they are stunned when I call them in because the aforementioned Supply Buyer somehow got ahold of the posting and was less than amused. Neither am I, especially since I just listened to a 45-minute lecture about how the ballpoint pens he orders are perfectly good and meet the same standards as the pricey non-generics.

Shifting gears a bit, no discussion about Social Media would be complete without some discussion about your posts in general. As of this writing the ethical use of social media in employment is still being debated, though the general consensus is that there is some protection afforded you and your online posts. I won't bore you with the intricacies of the NLRA and how online discussions have been interpreted as being protected under it, but I will tell you that making statements on Twitter such as "it is a beautiful day out, and I am stuck inside wack Acme company" is ill-advised. While your employer certainly may agree that it is a beautiful day, they may not agree with your assessment that the company is "wack," and even if they did, I am fairly certain they would rather their employees not advertise such feelings over the internet. Sure, it may be what is known as a protected activity, but I doubt it is going to win you many friends in higher places.

Is all this to say that you should pull down your pictures from the Beta Beta Beta beer pong championship?

Yes.

Does it mean that you shouldn't post stuff on your online profile where you are having a good time?

Maybe.

It is OK to have fun and the pictures to prove it, but be cautious that you don't do anything that could put your company in a bad light. For instance, if you are going to a wet t-shirt contest, don't wear the t-shirt you got in the orientation basket.

In other words, use common sense.

Oh, the places you'll go!

There is something alluring about the open road. Great books and not-so-great movies have all worked to romanticize the road for us; which helps explain why it seems that everyone wants a job where they travel. That is until they have a job that requires extensive travel. Don't get me wrong, frequent travel definitely has its advantages. For instance, I have collected enough portable shampoo bottles to cover me through a zombie apocalypse. I might be fending off the undead, but I will do so without fear of flakes.

But even if you don't land a job that takes you on the road 50 weeks out of the year, there is still a good chance you are going to have to travel some. So, I am going to present a few ideas that I have picked up either from my own experience working as a road warrior or from talking with my fellow frequent fliers.

Less is more

First off, if you are traveling for 3 days, how many pairs of shoes do you need to take with you? The pair on your feet will probably suffice, and maybe another pair for exercise. That's it, that is all you need. I know, I'm a guy and things are different for women, I get that (really, I don't, but I will pretend) but truth be told, a little planning will go a long way. It is easy to start getting ready for a business trip and find yourself thinking of all the contingencies: you may have to go out for a nice dinner, or there may be a lot of standing, or there might be a lot of walking, or you are going to have to wear a certain uniform, or whatever. When you find yourself doing this, stop. Your goal when packing for a trip is to fit (i.e. cram) your stuff in as small a suitcase as you can get your hands on, i.e. that will fit in the overhead bin. Once you get into this habit, you'll be glad you did. If you have to travel with a suit (which requires its own garment bag), can you wear it on the plane, then hang it up as soon as you are at the hotel? If you think it will get too wrinkled that way, trust me, it ain't got nothing over the luggage bay or even the overheads.

The same goes for pretty much everything else. Make it a goal to travel with as little stuff as you can get away with. Have a Kindle and an iPad? Get the Kindle app for your iPad. Got a bunch of magazines to read? Cut the articles out and put them in a folder, or scan them to read on your e-reader.

Prepare for the worse

With the first rule in mind, there are going to be times where you have to check your bag, either because you are taking a long trip, or you are toting some additional stuff that is needed for the trip. It happens, I get it. I'm not going to judge, though take my advice: always pack a carry-on with one complete change of clothes and your essentials. What are essentials? In my case is a toothbrush and travel size toothpaste, deodorant, and contact case (I don't mess with the solution, I can use tap water in a pinch), and a pair of undies. Everything else I can get from the hotel or even the airport.

Travel is unpredictable, and you do not know 100% when you are going to end up arriving, and what will be with you when you do. Sure, you may have a flight that is set to arrive at 3:00 in the afternoon, so if you forget something you will have time to make a stop, but flights are delayed and you may find yourself at your hotel at 9:00 at night, miles from a store that will sell you a spare pair of skivvies or a stick of deodorant. Most hotels can provide you with most of these essentials, but let's just say I wouldn't chance it. If you are prepared, you can always put off worrying about that until the next day.

Keep an electronics survival kit

You will find that there are few things worse than traveling only to find that you have a dead cell phone battery. Whatever you consider essential for travel: iPhone/Android/flip phone, iPad, Kindle, whatever; chances are that you can find a USB cable that will charge it. Couple that with a small portable battery pack and a small USB plug, and you are good to go. Now you can charge anywhere: hotel, conference, meeting, car, taxi, poolside. Where you keep this kit is entirely up to you, but I keep mine in my day bag since a lot of my travel is simple day trips. If you do it right, this shouldn't take up much space, but if your commuter bag is a little tight as it is, it might make sense to keep this in the above-referenced overnighter. The point is, there are few things that you can make your life more miserable on the road than a dead cell phone.

When packing, just roll with it.

Some years ago, I read an article about travel tips. One thing that jumped out at me was to roll your clothes to save space. I have to admit it took me a minute to believe that would really help, but it does. What you do is take your clothes and group them by what you are going to wear, putting those things that you care least about wrinkling (like socks and underwear) on top, meaning they are on the inside of the roll. You then simply roll these into tight rolls and set them in your bag. Then when you get where you are going, you just unroll and you are done. This isn't to say that you will not have any wrinkle issues, you are still going to want to hang stuff up as soon as you can, but if it is done right, it really does minimize the wrinkles and maximize space. Now keep in mind, until you get the hang of it, this system will result in some wrinkled clothes. I find it works well when traveling with polo-style shirts, or "wrinkle free" pants. For dress shirts, or dress slacks, these are going to need to be kept folded and laid over the top of your rolled clothes. In addition to cutting down on space, this also helps keep your socks and underwear organized, which is a whole other benefit.

Join every frequent traveler program you can, then stick with one

Your company may have some preferences when it comes to what hotels, airlines, and car rental companies you use. They may have exclusive arrangements, or they may have certain groups that you have to stay within. If that is the case your search should be pretty easy. Get in on it as soon as you book your first trip. Also, often times in these cases as an incentive to the company, the vendor will upgrade your membership which is always nice. Even if they don't, find brands you like, join their frequent traveler club and then stick with them.

So, what if your company has an exclusive agreement with a less than posh hotel chain? I say, don't knock it. You usually don't have to use the points for free nights there, but instead turn them into airline points, or exchange them for gift cards. I worked for a company that had an exclusive agreement with a particular hotel chain that fit into this category. In fact, the truth is, more than half of these hotels (and I use the term loosely) were situated behind a Denny's. That didn't stop me from joining their program though and taking advantage of whatever perks I could glean from them, which included free nights at some halfway decent properties. Bottom line here, if you have to stay there, make the most of it. If you have some level of free reign with your travel or not, try to find a chain that you like and stick with it, then watch the points add up.

Other things to look for in a frequent traveler program:

- Do the points expire?

This may sound like a bad thing, but if you travel regularly this can be to your benefit because often programs where the points expire more rapidly actually collect points more quickly. Of course, if you don't travel much, it really isn't going to do you a lot of good.

- Can you get extra points through other programs?

   The most obvious of this is credit cards and frequent flier programs, but you'd be surprised what all is out there.
- How long does it take to get to preferred status?

   Especially with frequent flier programs, this is a nice perk. Once you reach preferred status you can often bypass lines, get free upgrades, and accumulate points faster. It also works with hotels and rental cars as well.

- Who are their "partners?"

   Take a look to see what your options are for redeeming points. Like I mentioned earlier, there are other benefits besides free nights or travel. This can be especially useful if your company has an agreement with The Roach Motor Inn.

One final word on these programs: while I have yet to run into a company that requires you to use your frequent flier points for business use, you should still be aware of your company's policies all the same. A free night in at the Redneck Riviera in Destin might be a nice treat, but it might land you in hot water if your points are supposed to be used for business travel.

"That's how we've always done it, duh!"

I know what you are thinking; "here's the part where he goes on a rant and tells me to rid this from my vocabulary because it is a piss-poor excuse for being afraid to think outside of the box."

If that is what you think, you are part-right. I do want you to rid it from your vocabulary, but not because it is a cop-out. In reality, it is often true and honestly it is not always bad, there may be a very good reason why you have always done it this way.

Rid it from your vocabulary because it will get you in trouble. No one wants to hear that phrase when you are asked why you do something a certain way. Instead say, "I am not sure why we do it this way, that is how I was taught." Or, if you find yourself in the unenviable situation of defending an action of a superior or someone else who happens to be wielding power at the moment, say "I wasn't aware that there was anything wrong with doing it this way, I've never been told otherwise."

Now let's be honest for a moment about this illustrious phrase. I have found that in many, make that most, instances the biggest critics of this phrase don't like it because it impedes their ability to implement a way of doing something that more than likely they utilized at their previous company; which they were more comfortable with. In other words, they want to do it the way they have always done it...

Of course, the best way to avoid the phrase that shall not be mentioned is to do your homework and ask questions. If you are shown how to do something, ask whoever showed you why they do it this way. Yes, some people are going to get uncomfortable, because no one wants to answer with "because that is how we've always done it," though more than a few will be thinking it and many more will come right out and say it anyway. Therefore, be sensitive in your approach and say, "that's OK, I just want to understand the process thoroughly." This can be the difference from being seen as judgmental turd versus someone who genuinely cares about the organization and the people who helped build it.

Privacy is dead

You have no doubt heard the warning to be careful what you put out on social media. In fact, we just talked about this earlier. Twitter, Facebook, blogs, etc., are open to anyone. An entire industry has sprung up that helps companies manage their online profile. Maybe someday that will trickle down to individuals, but until it does, or it becomes affordable, it is up to us to manage our own online profiles.

This issue goes beyond social media, though. If you have a computer at your desk, you probably don't have to look far to find some indication that the machine doesn't belong to you, maybe it is a metal bar code, or the name of the computer itself, or a lack of "SysAdmin rights," whatever. In addition, if your company has a handbook or any kind of company policy, there is likely some verbiage making it clear that the equipment and anything on said equipment is the company's. If you haven't figured it out by now, this means that no matter what you have on that computer, it is the property of your employer and not you. So, if you think that you have the cure for cancer, but need to type up the notes, do it when you get home.

The main issue comes when people decide to use their work computers to save pictures from this year's Halloween party where they decided to dress as a French Maid (sorry Larry, it was going to come out sooner or later). Or maybe they think they are a budding poet so they decide to work on their prose while sitting at their desk during lunch – the problem is that they are one of those nasty poets. Maybe they decide to watch that inappropriate YouTube video their buddy sent along earlier involving a duck, a golf ball, and a bodybuilder wearing house shoes. While most companies do not make a habit of looking at everyone's e-mail or scanning the web pages that you look at, the fact is that in most cases they have every right to do so. Play it safe and keep work and personal separate.

Use technology to control your image

Technology is a tool and therefore is there to make our jobs easier as well as make us more efficient (remind yourself of this as you play that latest $0.99 wonder from the app store).

So why don't we utilize the subtleties of technology? For example, let's say that you are sitting at home watching TV and while you are at it you decide to peck out a couple of e-mails during the commercials. It's not like you have to do it, you are just staying one step ahead. So, you type the message and then you hit send. What kind of message are you actually sending?

Is it:

"Hey guys, I am sitting here watching Jimmy Fallon and thought I would respond to a couple of notes really quick,"

- or -

"Hey everyone, it's me. I have so much work that I can't get it all done during the day so I am sitting here burning the midnight oil... again."

Of course, the vast majority of the time no one is going to think anything of it one way or the other, but by hitting send right away you could be missing a great opportunity.

Instead of typing and sending, why not type, save, and send first thing in the morning when you are back at the office. Your recipients think that while everyone else was getting their coffee and yakking about the show you were watching while you typed the note, it looks like you were actually working.

Of course, in today's world of tablet computers and smartphones, the game changes a little bit, but the principle still holds true. If the email is a quick yes or no response, that is one thing. But if you are actually wrapping something up, go ahead and do it and just wait to hit send until you are actually back at the office.

There is also a flip side. Your boss or some of your internal customers may value late night hard work. They themselves may not see it as being overwhelmed, but rather as strong work ethic that better mirrors their own. If you are responding to a note from one of those people, don't wait, send the note right then from your computer if possible. The font is usually different than from a phone or tablet, so it will look like you were actually working and not, in fact, responding while waiting for someone to take your order at Sushi Heaven. Another way to work with these types of people is to type, save, and send later. Let's say that you are typing a note to one of these workaholics at say 3:30 in the afternoon. If it is an e-mail, chances are it is not absolutely urgent, so it can wait until later that night, as in during a commercial break. Save it to drafts and when Jimmy Fallon tells you that he will be right back, boot up the old trusty laptop, pull up your draft(s) and start sending. From boot up to shut down, you'll probably be finished before they are back to your regularly scheduled program, yet you'd be surprised at how much this can endear you to your customers.

Let me give you an example. I once worked at a company where several high-ranking folks were of that mentality. I had just gone on vacation with my wife and as she was getting ready for bed, I thought I would send out a quick note I had drafted to one of these folks earlier that day. I had my laptop with me so I booted up and hit send. When I was back from vacation there was a glowing commendation from this individual about how refreshing it is to know that there are others who work as hard as she does. It took me all of 2 minutes but had a huge positive impact, and all of the sudden I was endeared to this high-ranking executive. To her, I was one of the hard-working elite when in reality there simply wasn't anything on TV in my hotel room.

Now, having said that, I know I am probably going to get angry letters telling me that I should not advocate taking your computer on vacation, it is not a vacation if you are working, and I agree wholeheartedly: you have to separate, shut down, unplug. In other words, enjoy yourself. That said, I never leave home without some way to connect to my office, even if only with my iPhone. Nothing ruins a vacation like remembering something you needed to do, and knowing there is nothing you can do until you get back... So just so we are clear: being ABLE to connect to work and STAYING CONNECTED to work are two entirely different things. Don't misunderstand me, and save the angry letters for someone else.

Know your audience

This chapter goes along closely with using technology to control your image. This is especially important if you work in an industry that has people working in different environments than you. For example, I have spent a good deal of my professional life working in the corporate headquarters of a large retailer. It didn't take long to realize that not all the people I worked with held the same hours that I did. Being retail, the stores did most of their business over weekends, holidays, and evenings. Being a corporate environment, the office kept traditional office hours. This dichotomy helped foster the general perception that the corporate people didn't work as hard as the store folks did, which often manifest in 5:15 pm emails or voice messages with comments like: "I know you are gone for the day, but can you give me a call tomorrow?"

I quickly saw this as a great opportunity to stand out. I returned those calls after 5:00 (or at least a lot of them), though admittedly not always from the office. I had these really cool devices, you might have heard of them, they are called a cell phone and a Bluetooth headset. I made calls on the way home, or even when I got home. I'm talking about 10 – 15 minute calls where instead of listening to the radio, I talked with someone. It took nothing away from my free time, but in doing so I quickly got the reputation as someone who puts in the hours and soon I became one of "them."

In HR, many of my fellow practitioners have a reputation for being a stickler for processes and not understanding the business units they support. That has never worked for me, which is why I often hear "you are not like other HR people I've worked with." Do I throw the rules away? Of course not, but I do look for alternatives; ways to show that I am a true business partner and that I deserve the trust that my partners have given me. It may be a little more work, but I take the time to think about what is important to those businesses that I support, and then adjust accordingly.

Am I perfect?

Of course I am.

Ok, maybe not, but I will say that I have never been accused of being like a typical HR guy, and based on the reputation that Human Resources has earned, that is not a bad thing.

If you take this approach of looking at things from the eyes of those you work with, regardless of whether they have sway or not, your street cred will get a nice boost.

Perception is reality

You may be the smartest guy in the department. You may know more than anyone else on your floor and be the hardest working person in the office, but...

You come to work dressed like you just rolled out of bed. When you go into your boss' office, you slouch into the chair, don't make eye contact, habitually ask to borrow a pen when she gives you directions because you left yours at your desk, and then write the instructions on your hand because, oh yeah, you left your notepad at your desk as well. What do you think your boss thinks of you?

So, what's the takeaway? Take a step back and look at yourself through the eyes of your boss, or her boss:

- Do you look like someone who is eager to come to work?
- Do you look like someone who is interested in making the company grow?
- Do you look like someone who is passionate about their career?
- Do you look like someone that is going to make your boss look good if she puts you in front of her boss?

A few things to think about right away:

Consider your body language and your appearance. Do you come across as someone who is interested? Someone who cares about the job? Or do you reek of slacker?

How do you handle the little things? Do you promptly respond to voicemails? E-mails? Do you greet people in the halls? Do you show genuine appreciation for the work that others do?

I once worked with a Marketing Executive who was actually pretty good at what she did. The problem was she spent what seemed like a whole lot of time using her position to meet with the celebrities that the company got endorsements from. She was always the first to take tickets for herself and her family that were presented from various media outlets and rarely shared them with other members of her team. This earned her the nickname within her department of Gimme-Ginny (her name and the subsequent nickname has been changed). How do you think Gimme-Ginny's career ended up? I'm not sure, I lost track of her when she left the company. She was very talented, had a tremendous amount of potential, and I honestly believe that she was truly interested in helping the company grow. None of that mattered, though because of how she was perceived.

Don't make the same mistake, instead take time to self-reflect. Use your journal to write out observations you have about how others act around you, and give yourself an honest look. Does it seem like people are avoiding you? Do you find yourself apologizing for not responding to email quickly? Do people make offhand comments like "I thought of scheduling that for 8:00, but wasn't sure you'd be able to make it," or "Wow! You answered your phone! There's a first." These are all gifts if you use them. If you listen to what people are saying you can correct behaviors or even swing the pendulum to the other side. You can be better.

The world may be your oyster, but you are always in a fish bowl

As you rise through the ranks, you may find that there are more eyes on you than you are used to. Some of these folks are going to be looking for guidance, which is kind of cool if you think about it. On the flip side, there are going to be those looking for you to screw up. These are the people who think they are just as good as you are, perhaps even better. It is more than petty jealousy though, these same folks often also think that you are the only thing standing between them and the next level, or they may feel that you took the promotion that was rightfully theirs.

These people are easy to recognize. They are the ones who say things like "I've been here as long as Joe, and yet he's making more than me." Or, "this company only promotes brown-nosers... I'd have been promoted a long time ago if I were willing to plant my lips on [The Boss'] butt." Or, "she only got that because of office politics." These folks make these statements because they know, at least on a subconscious level, that the reason they have not had the same level of success as others is because they are unwilling to make the necessary changes and sacrifices needed to make them promotable. Maybe it is a lack of willingness to put in the extra hours, or they are just not willing to take on the extra responsibilities. Maybe they are not able to relocate, or maybe they just aren't as smart as the other guy. Whatever the case, they are unwilling to look in the mirror, find and own up to the deficiency and at least try and address whatever the problem is. This is not to say that people don't get ahead by planting their lips firmly on the backside of a higher-up, but these people very quickly find themselves over their heads and thus their rise is usually short-lived.

So, what does all this mean to you? At some point, probably soon, you are going to find yourself in a situation where you are defending your status and rank.
Remember, these people are usually cowards and will not attack you head on, instead they will build a group of like-minded lemmings to follow in their wake and will engage in Guerrilla Office Warfare, with tactics including:

- Murmuring behind your back
- Dropping little hints to their bosses that you aren't worth your salt, and
- Dropping subtle little hints to your boss. Things like, "I would have gone to Jim, but it just seems that he has been SO overwhelmed lately, I don't want to add something else to his plate..."

How do you combat this? How do you fight this type of war on your career? You set the standard on every front.

- Be the example
- Stay cool and calm under pressure, and
- Be careful who you confide in

The thing is, all this goes against our human tendencies. I mean we are under attack, dammit! We need to go on the offensive! We need to take the fight to them! While that may be gratifying, it hardly ever ends well for you, and whoever you are going up against is usually validated. Talk about a lose-win situation.

It's not ALL about the money, honey

During my long and storied tenure in HR, I have seen a fair number of careers take a slight detour, if not a sharp turn over a couple of grand in salary. Someone is offered an opportunity to take on some additional career building opportunities, and they see this as a chance to pad their wallets. "Sure, I can do that," they say with a smile, "but I'm going to need an extra $2,000 since I'm going to be taking on this additional responsibility."

How do you think the manager feels about this? Are they going to see you as someone who genuinely wants to further their career? Are you someone that is going to be top of mind for the next opportunity?

There's a reason why you don't enter into an interview and start talking about money right off; you want to project to the decision makers that you are excited about the opportunity. So why would this be any different? The objective is to snag the opportunity, and then show them what you are capable of. Show them that you are indispensable. Show them that you are worth more than the 3 grand you would have asked for.

"But what if they don't come through? I just got shorted 3G's that I might have snagged otherwise." True, but this is not a sprint, it's a marathon. If they don't come through on their own, what makes you think that they aren't going to make up for it at review time? Or bonus time? On the flip side who's to say that they aren't going to come back with 5 grand after a couple of months? Negotiations are always a gamble and remember that there are two sides of the table. Worst case scenario, you find that what you think you bring to the company is less than what the company does. If this is the case you can either prove your value, which may mean working for another boss, or you can find another company that agrees with the value you bring to the organization. You can't always play it safe, but this is a pretty small risk in the overall scheme of things.

I can speak to this personally. I was just starting out in Human Resources, working in Benefits. At the time, the company I was working for had one Recruiter, and he was nearing retirement. My goal at that time was to become an HR Generalist, which is to say someone who touches all parts of HR and then move into a management role. At the time, the HR Department was all of 6 people, myself included. When the Recruiter retired, The HR Director approached me and asked me to take over this person's responsibilities. Seeing this as a way to broaden my experience, I jumped at the chance, despite the fact that she told me I would continue in my Benefits role as well. Essentially, she wanted me to literally do two jobs and there was no discussion of a pay increase. Still, I was on cloud nine. I was now a recruiter and one step closer to my goal. Sure, I would have liked a few extra dollars, but I was in it for the long game. When review time came around I received a 20% pay increase. Within a year I was promoted again, and two years later my salary had almost doubled. Had I unfurled my hand and demanded immediate compensation for taking on the role, I could have reasonably expected a 5-10% bump up front, and the standard 3% come review time. That second promotion would have been a little further down the horizon if it had happened at all.

You have to put yourself in the manager's shoes because their success will largely impact yours. Do you want someone who is there for a paycheck, or someone who is excited about the work? Who is going to do a better job and lift you, the manager, up?

Office politics (ain't necessarily bad)

I love it when people talk about "Office Politics." It usually comes up when someone tells me that someone got a promotion, better desk, certain perk, or something else that they wanted. I have never been privy to a conversation where anyone says, "oh, that was just office politics," and the other person says, "cool! I love office politics." The fact is, office politics is a typical cop-out as to why one person got a promotion, or office, or window spot, or whatever, whereas the other person didn't. I say this is a cop-out because what the person who feels slighted calls "office politics" is really the result of someone else's better work ethic, positive attitude, resourcefulness, or another trait that the boss values. It is easier to blame office politics than to say "I was up for this promotion, but the fact is, I suck at the skills that they needed." So, we block this out and look for something else to blame. Of course, office politics isn't the only scapegoat out there. If the beneficiary of the good fortune also happens to be attractive, there is always that...

None of this is to say that office politics do not exist, nor am I so naïve as to think they don't affect careers. I have seen a fair share of talented people miss out on promotions or cherry projects simply because they were out-politicked. Sometimes life just isn't fair.

Politics has really gotten a bad rap over the years, but it really does serve a purpose. Essentially, politics is little more than the art of getting things done. It has been around as long as we as humans have banded together, and by extension, sought out someone to lead us. So, the way I see it, you have two choices: 1) play along, or 2) complain. Since you are reading this book, I assume that you are going to choose door number 1 and play along.

Since every organization is different, how you handle the politics of your organization depends on, well, the organization you are at and its unique politics. Good politics is like the difference between art and porn: you know it when you see it. So, when you see it, study it. Become friends with the masters, and remember: when it comes to politics one size does not fit all.

I once worked with a guy who noticed that at his previous job the key players arrived at work about thirty minutes early and drank coffee in the break room. It was an informal time that they could have friendly chats, as well as talk about the goings on within the company, initiatives and other things that could impact the company overall. So, my co-worker began coming in thirty minutes early as well. He sat in the break-room and visited with these people. This 30-minute investment gave him exposure to the key decision makers, provided him insight, and gave the impression that he was proactive. If he needed something done, instead of scheduling a meeting with the subordinate of a decision maker, he would bring it up casually to their honcho, get the buy-in and then let the pieces fall out from there. It was a very good strategy, and it worked well. So well, in fact, that he took it up at his next job, which is where I met him. The problem is, at the new job the culture was not one of get there early and chat. It's not that people didn't get there early, but those that did went straight to work and were in no mood for idle chit-chat. However, he was getting there early to chat with the higher-ups and the higher-ups either weren't there, or they saw him popping in and trying to chat with them as a distraction. What he should have done is hang around until 5:30 or even 6, when the only ones in the building were the executives and decision-makers, who were winding down and often were more willing to chat. I utilized the second strategy myself and had the same effect he had with his early arrivals at his previous company. When I suggested he change his approach, he said that he already got there early, why would he want to stay late as well? While I understand the sentiment, his whole reason for getting there early was to get face time with the decision makers, something he had lamented he wasn't getting here.

Another thing to remember about politics is that they are a tool, just like anything else that we have talked about here. If your boss and the executive team play golf, it is probably not a bad idea to learn to play golf. Just don't think that having a good swing is a substitute for knowing your stuff. Politics, even when used properly, will only get you so far.

Lastly, get ready for some nastiness, because politics can be cheap and dirty. People will talk about you behind your back, people will call you a kiss-up. People will say that you are sleeping with the boss (and this is not just if you are attractive, I have heard it about some very ugly folks too). Just remember that all of this is simply because it is easier to talk about someone than it is to admit that the person they are talking about is better than them.

It's not a popularity contest.
(Well, actually it kind of is)

Along the lines of politics, there is nothing wrong with being liked. Sure, as you rise in the organization you will find that fewer and fewer people are gunning for you, but that doesn't mean that you have to be a jerk either. You have to think of yourself as a commodity because quite simply that is what you are. The company hired you because they felt that you were the best product they could get for the money that they were willing to spend.
However, now that you are working, you have to constantly market yourself as the best thing since sliced bread. You have to show your future bosses that when they are looking in the pool of internal candidates for a peach role that you are the one that they want. Do you accomplish this by being a jerk? By being anti-social? By having a reputation for being difficult?

Decision makers are human too, and if they are looking for a Director to report to them, who are they going to pick? The sour personality with the "glass-half-empty" attitude, or the upbeat, almost bubbly, "glass-half-full" kind of guy?

Which one would you pick?

Think about this closely and then take a good look in the mirror. Where do you fit? Even if you think that you are friendly and nice, there is always room for improvement. An easy thing you can start doing right now is smile and say thank you to everyone who helps you, from the IT Director who does you a quick favor to the custodian who removes the trash from your cube every day. If you get a reputation for being well-liked, people tend to stand up for you when you are not around.

If you do this, people will talk about how friendly you are and how much they like working with you, or better yet, how they would like to work with you.

Why does this matter?

The more of these people who talk, the more likely they are going to get it in front of a decision maker. We all develop opinions about other people, whether we know the person or not. Have you ever, in conversation, made a statement to someone else that you don't know about another person only to have whomever you are talking with respond with "really? I don't feel that way at all..." What happens to your perception of that person?

I left a company I had been at for over 9 years to work in a different industry. I left for a number of reasons, but mostly because I saw it as the right career move for me. I had been at the company for just under 6 weeks when my former boss' boss called and asked me to come back. She told me, and I will never forget it, that the President told her to get me back. The President of the company. He was relatively new to the company, having only been in the post for a few months, and up to this point, I had only worked with him one time, before his promotion and it was not something that I thought went all that well, yet here he was telling this Executive Vice President not to call him back until I agreed to return. What caused this? Was it my excellent handling of the flood of four-letter words flying out of his mouth in sheer exasperation? Afraid not. The EVP and the President both told me later that it was the people in and around my department talking about how much I was missed. It was people talking either to him or within earshot of him, complimenting me and my personality. Oh, and did I mention I got a nice raise?

Even a snake can lead you to water

I am going to let you in on a secret: I hate snakes. I don't like the way they look, I don't like the way they feel, I just don't like them. I know some people do and bully for them – I will remember them in my prayers.

In addition to the actual cold-blooded, slithering, often venomous creatures that feed on rats, there are also certain people that meet enough criteria to qualify for this label as well. They know no gender, race, color, religion or creed. They come in all sizes and age is irrelevant, yet we usually know them when we see them, with our first instinct being to avoid them. They are usually selfish creatures, only looking out for themselves and trying to get an angle and often doing so at your expense.

But they can be useful as well.

I am not advocating that you become chums with these people and go to Arby's together every Tuesday, but don't write them off either. You see, even a snake at some point is going to need water and where they go to get it might come in handy for you. Throw them the occasional bone and they might feel the need to reciprocate, and when they do, you may be surprised to learn what they might give up.

Let me give you an example. I had started working at a new company and got a call from a contractor who was clearly looking to expand his reach into the organization. I had been warned by others that he was not to be trusted, so much so that he had actually almost derailed my efforts to join this organization. However, I also knew that he had some insight that could be useful, so I took his call. The insight I got was invaluable. Not only did he tell me more about my predecessor than I could have ever guessed, most of which turned out to be true. He gave me a ton of insight into my new boss, as well as the power players in the company. Within 20 minutes I knew more than I could have learned in 6 months.

All this said, one thing to keep in mind when dealing with these kinds of people: never forget that they are in it for themselves and will climb, or slither, on top of anyone they can in order to get to where they want to be.

This place sucks, signed: Anonymous

Have you ever worked anywhere that had a policy in their handbook that read something like this:

"At Acme Corp., we pride ourselves in knowing that our management team members are the best in the business and there is nothing that you can say that will change our point of view. Therefore, we are proud to have a Closed-Door Policy. If you have a complaint, just murmur about it amongst yourselves. Remember: you are lucky to have a job."

If you do in fact work for a company with this type of policy, please send me a copy: jim@hrforyall.com – I guarantee I can find a use for it.

While I joke about it, there are a whole lot of companies whose practices closely align with that statement, irrespective of what their employee handbook says. In fact, most companies out there have some type of Open Door policy, but that is usually not the actual practice. Even companies with true Open-Door policies rarely have managers who truly embrace it. Is that to say that they will fire you for going to their boss or HR? Not necessarily, but they may grade you harder on your next performance review, or overlook you when the next plum assignment comes along. Or it will be more subtle. Things like being less friendly to you, or less likely to go to bat for you.

Now before you start condemning them, put yourself in their shoes. Let's say you manage a division within your department and have 8 employees reporting to you. As Division Manager, you report to a Regional Director who reports to an Area Director, who reports to the VP of your Continent who reports to an EVP who reports to the CEO who reports to the Chairman of the Board who reports to 3 million stockholders. One of your employees, a Widget Data Analyst, sends an e-mail to your Area Director saying that she requested time off for her birthday and it has not been approved. She goes on to say that you gave Sandy time off for her birthday and therefore surmises that you have not approved her time off because you are upset at her for pointing out a misspelling in a memo you asked her to proof before you sent it out to the other Division Managers (you called them Division **Mangers**). She goes on to say that she feels like you really never did like her because when you say good morning it is only half-hearted, and usually while you are sipping your coffee, a gesture that she is sure is a sign of disrespect in some cultures.

Of course, that is just her side. Let's now look at what she left out: 1.) Her birthday is Thursday, which is when you are expecting a major replenishment order to come in which needs to be redistributed before the weekend, a task that is core to her job. 2.) Mandatory training is going on that day and half the department is going to be out (thank you, HR). 3.) She e-mailed the request for time off on Friday at 4:45, and today is Monday... Combine all that with the fact you have spent the better part of the morning reconfiguring work duties to ensure that everything is covered when she does go out on her birthday. Oh, and you were just one line short of sending off the e-mail approving the time off before you were interrupted by your boss calling, wondering why her boss, that is your boss' boss, just received a note from your employee wondering about time off...

Remember, you are the Division Manager for this employee. You know that you cannot treat her differently and besides, you are in the process of approving the vacation anyway. Still, what is your feeling towards this employee at this precise moment? If you aren't at least slightly pissed off, you very well may be a sociopath.

So, what is the moral of this story? Never go above your boss' head? No. If that were the case, people like me would be out of a job and we'd be relegated to hawking books about getting ahead in today's workforce.

If you do need to go above your boss' head, make sure it is not only your last resort but also that you have thought it through completely. In other words, when you are certain you have exhausted all other options, or when there are simply no other options available to you, then talk with them. For instance, if your boss is telling you that the only way you are going to get ahead is if you start wearing short skirts, low cut blouses and start staying late on Wednesday nights when his wife is out late playing poker with her friends, then I don't know if you have a lot of other options.

But barring the obvious illegal, immoral and unethical situations, what are your other options? Well, there is always the anonymous complaint. In your mind, this will: a.) get the boss' attention (maybe, maybe not) b.) allow you to remain under the radar (maybe, maybe not) and c.) ensure the complaint is taken seriously (again: maybe, maybe not).

Like any other form of communication, an anonymous complaint's effectiveness essentially comes down to what is being said. If your complaint is something to the effect of: "my boss is a big fat know-it-all who has no respect for his employees," don't expect a full-scale assault from the HR department. If the complaint reads somewhere along the lines of "my boss is stealing from the company. I saw him open the petty cash safe by himself, pull money out, put it in his pocket and close the safe back without signing any money out, as per company procedure." That is more likely to be looked into a little bit more carefully. Even then, when you forgo your name and/or signature, you forgo a level of trust in the complaint.

One final thought on notes to boss' bosses. Unless you are going the anonymous route, I would strongly recommend that you e-mail the note and bcc it back to yourself and print the bcc note out for safe keeping. I recommend this because in the event that things do get shaky for you, you'll at least have proof that you made a complaint **before** the retaliation started. I know this goes slightly counter to my chapter on covering your ass(ets), but in this case, it might be prudent to not put it out there quite so blatantly.

That's it, I quit!

It's inevitable: at some point in your career you are going to hear, see, or otherwise sense something that you don't like. When this happens, you may even be tempted to threaten to quit if something doesn't change. They will see that you mean business, and someone with your knowledge, understanding, and general good looks is all but irreplaceable.

Don't bet the farm on it.

I have been presented with the threat of someone quitting more times than I can count, and my usual response is "I accept your resignation." The person on the other end is usually shocked by this and often stammers back that they didn't mean to quit; they were just upset.

Often times, this is too bad, so sad. If you are going to throw that out there, you had better be prepared for the real possibility that the person on the other end might not value you as much as you think.

The same goes for other statements – "I'll sue," or "I'll get a lawyer." Unless you are working with an attorney at that very moment and he or she has advised you to make that statement – don't. If you are working with an attorney and they advise you to make that statement, you might want to look for another one.

The fact is, if you do have a case and you are genuinely owed or entitled to something, rarely does anything good come from showing your cards. By contrast, when you make a legal threat like that, most people simply close up and refuse to talk. After all, why should they try and work with you when all you are going to do is take them to court anyway?

Dealing with the office bully without punching them in the nose

When you were growing up did you ever know someone who was a bully? Maybe you were one yourself at some point or another. The stereotypical bully was someone who picked on younger and/or smaller kids, giving them wedgies and stealing their lunch money, but that is only a small portion of what truly happens in bullying situations. Bullying is often a mob mentality; it often happens when the bully is able to rally others behind them and turn those numbers against someone who is perceived as weaker, either socially or physically. Bullying has always been around and the truth is it does not go away as we get older. In fact, chances are you have seen bullying in some form or fashion in the real world today, perhaps in the form of online trolls or simply someone intentionally not being invited to lunch.

While bullying is less obvious as we grow older, it still occurs, and the hard truth is you will likely work with, or for, someone who is nothing short of a bully. So how do you spot them and, more importantly, deal with them?

While bullies at work rarely look like the cartoonish characters they are portrayed to be, in my observation they do tend to share traits from a fairly large pool:

- Work bullies are often promoted rapidly within the organization without a lot of formal supervisory training. One of the biggest challenges I think organizations face today is the knee-jerk reaction to promote the best performing widget-maker to supervisor, without any thought to how they are going to manage the other widget makers, and compounding this by not taking the time and making the investment to formally train them on how to properly supervise others.

- Work bullies are often in fear of their jobs. Frequently they are afraid that their job will be the next one eliminated. Even if there are no layoffs on the horizon and the company is doing well, they will tell you that it is coming and you need to be ready.
- Bullies tend to be very competitive. Whether it is a disagreement over how a company policy should be interpreted or horseshoes at the department picnic, they hate to lose.
- Almost without question, they have very big egos.

Now all of these are not, in and of themselves, bad traits to have. In fact, as you read it, you are probably seeing some of yourself in one of these statements. You don't have to look very far to see some very high-ranking people in your organization who also exhibit one, or more of these traits. The difference is that in almost all cases, the people who are successful (read: not bullies) have one additional trait that the bullies don't: strong self-esteem.

I have never met a bully, in the schoolyard or the workplace, who genuinely had good self-esteem. I suppose this is why they became bullies. We all want to feel good about ourselves, if you have strong self-esteem and know that you are good, make that damn good, at what you do you don't need to bring others down to lift yourself up. Instead, you are going to take your competitive nature and use it to build up those around you, whether it is a team you are leading, your peers, or your boss.

Are you fearful of your job? Maybe so, but not to the point that you are worried that you are going to get laid off or eliminated at every turn. Instead, you hold the job in such high regard you do not want to let it, or your employer, down. You know how it can be and you are striving to push it beyond where it is right now. There might be others out there who may be able to come in, take your job and do it better than you, but the difference between you and the bully is that you channel your fear back into the job and make it better.

So, what do you do when you have to interact with a bully? The same thing you were taught when you were growing up: you stand up to them. However, unlike the schoolyard where you stood toe-to-toe and told them to bugger off, you will need to be a little more diplomatic.

If you were like me and ever stood up to a bully in the schoolyard you might have gone home with a black eye. It hurt and people stared for a few days until it healed (the raw meat thing never seemed to help me) but after that, it was over and the bully had moved on to someone else. In the workplace, the black eye may stay with you a little longer if you aren't careful. When you stand up to the office bully, you have to approach it from a professional standpoint and turn whatever it is they are dangling in front of you back on them.

My first real encounter with a workplace bully was right out of college. I was one of two assistant managers, but unlike my peer, I was offered the job right out of college. Not having a college degree, she had worked her way into the position and because of her job knowledge and work ethic she had rightfully earned the respect of the team. When I came on I was told early on that this was her shop and I would do best to stay out of her way. The only difference in our business cards was our names (for the sake of example, we'll call her Tabitha) and we had equal authority within the building. However, she often made statements to the effect that if I didn't do this, or if I didn't do that, I would be fired. I was new and she certainly had a team of followers so I did as I was told, essentially giving her my professional "lunch money." Then one day an employee approached me. "Jim," he said, "I like you and that is why I am telling you this. You need to stop doing X, or you are going to get fired." I was shocked, 'X' was a project assigned to me by my District Manager, who was not just mine and Tabitha's boss, but our boss' boss. In other words, I wasn't about to stop doing that project unless I was told my District Manager do so. I thanked the employee and moved on, but then it hit me – Tabitha had been telling others in the group that she had authority over me to the point that she could fire me. Not "get me fired," as in going to my boss, but actually fire me. Now I would not be worth my HR salt if I didn't tell you I should have gone to our boss or to my Human Resources person, or some other avenue, but the truth be told, sometimes it just ain't that easy. In this situation, by doing that I would have alienated myself from the team – those employees who followed and looked up to her. So, I resolved to confront her at my first opportunity, which came rather quickly. She made a comment, I honestly can't recall what it was, but essentially, she threatened my job. Not only that but in typical bully fashion, she did it in front of a crowd. I looked at her and said, "OK, I guess Tom (our boss) will have to fire me. She stood firm when she said "no, Tom doesn't know anything about this. It is between you and me." I replied that I had nothing to worry about because she couldn't fire me. She stammered a little, told me that Tom would do what she said, walked away, and that was the last time that she threatened my job. Did it get easier after that? Yes. Did I invite her to my house for dinner? Nope. Don't be mistaken, that wasn't the last time that she tried to intimidate me, but I was ready after that. I always had a business reason for what I was doing, I always covered my bases and I never stooped to her level of threats.

When it comes to workplace bullies, you cannot fight fire with fire. You have to fight with business logic and reasoning.

Bad bosses and oppressive regimes

Houston's old NFL franchise, the Houston Oilers, had their share of colorful coaches back in the day, but I dare say none holds a place in the hearts of long-term Houstonians like Bum Phillips, a legendary coach known as much for his one-offs as for his coaching. While I moved to Houston well after the Oiler days, that isn't to say I haven't heard my share of "Luv Ya Blue" stories. One such story came after he was released from the Houston Oilers. At that time, he was quoted as saying "there are two kinds of professional football coaches: them that have been fired, and them that are going to be fired."

That truism extends beyond the world of coaching professional football. I would expand upon that to say that "there are two kinds of employees: them that have worked for bad bosses, and them that are going to work for bad bosses."

If you have never worked for a bad boss, fantastic! Just remember, there will come a time when you will remember that good boss fondly as you suffer under the SOB you will invariably be working for in the future.

To understand a bad boss, I think it is important to get to the root cause of why they are bad in the first place. Just as leaders are made not born, bad bosses don't come into the world with a predisposed genetic configuration that ensures they will someday be a completely incompetent manager, or at the bare minimum a jerk to their employees. They are formed in the womb of the business world; a product of their own bad bosses, poorly executed career development, and a library devoid of books such as the one you are reading now.

So, what to do with a truly bad boss?

You aren't going to like this, but in most cases, the best thing to do is wait them out. I have worked for my share of bad bosses: people who were completely incompetent, who were clearly only concerned with getting ahead and not at all concerned with the company's goals. I have worked with bosses who were promoted over their heads and bosses who I could only describe as arrogant. The one thing I can say about most of my bad bosses is that, just like oppressive regimes, they eventually fell. It may have taken a while, but eventually, the people who report to them had enough and revolted.

Unfortunately, in many instances, just as with an oppressive regime, the boss will not go down without a fight. As we have seen over and over again when the people of a country decide to step up and take a stand against an oppressive dictator, there is usually bloodshed. Sometimes this works to keep the regime in place, but often times it only works to galvanize support for the opposition. In the business world, this equates to turnover; as though the manager is standing in front of his direct reports and declares: "the firings will continue until morale improves."

So, what are some strategies that work to alleviate the problem before you become part of the "morale improvement program?"

There is really only one: talk to your boss. Remember that regardless of how big of a prick the boss is being, they are human and driven by human needs. If they feel that they are being threatened, things might get hairy. In these situations, it is usually best to walk in, close the door, lay it out on the table, and rationally explain to them how they are being perceived.

There are two key points I want you to pull from this. First is the rational part. I'm not just talking about remaining calm, though that is important, I'm talking about giving them facts, not estimates or broad statements. "You are a complete jerk," is a broad statement. It may be true, but it is still broad. What are they doing? What behavior are they exhibiting? Instead say: "you know Jim, you have a tendency to cut people off when they are talking." That is something they can address and refrain from doing going forward.

The second thing to pull from the phrase is the part about being perceived. No matter how much we like to say to the contrary, no one likes criticism. Almost everyone takes it as a personal attack. By telling them that they are being perceived a certain way essentially tells them that you do not think they mean to come across the way they are. Essentially you are giving them the benefit of the doubt. Back to my earlier critique, instead of "you are a complete jerk," instead you say "you know Jim, you have a tendency to cut people off when they are talking. That gives the perception that you don't care about what they are saying." No one in a leadership role wants to be perceived this way, so they are more likely to take the feedback and apply it.

Once you have the conversation, record it. E-mail it to yourself or store it somewhere that it will have a definitive timestamp. If the behavior continues then take it up the ladder or to HR.

Caveat: There are may be instances where talking to the boss just isn't enough. If they are engaged in, or trying to engage in, criminal or socially reprehensible behavior like stealing, or threatening your job in exchange for sexual favors, for example, it is probably best to skip the chat and go straight to their boss or Human Resources.

The new dog has to pee on every tree

I am a dog person. That is not to say that I do not like cats, I just can't eat a whole one by myself.

Ok, bad joke.

There have been very few times in my life when I didn't have a dog, and as anyone who has been around dogs of the male variety knows, when they enter a new yard or go for a walk, or whatever, the first priority is to mark their territory by peeing on virtually every tree.

New people are like this as well. When someone starts in a new role, especially one of authority, often their first objective is to make an impression as quickly as possible. This usually does not involve urinating on other people's desks, file cabinets, and other office furniture, though admittedly my years in HR have made me somewhat numb to surprise. Instead, it usually involves seemingly "big" changes, often with roles and the people who are in them. If you are part of a group where this is happening, it can be annoying at the very least, but what can you do about it?

Usually, nothing. Unless someone is actually peeing on your desk, at which point you should notify your HR contact immediately.

In the case of the other, more common situation, it is best to not only let them do it but provide as much support as possible and never, EVER say "this isn't how we have done this before." Remember, they are not only peeing on the trees, they are looking around to see who is with them. They are looking to see who is trying to go back and pee over their mark once they have walked away. Don't be that person, be a supporter instead. Who knows, they might just have some good ideas. Even if all of their grand ideas don't work, they usually need to see it for themselves and not hear why it isn't going to work from you.

The thing is, just like dogs, once they have peed on all the trees they usually move on unless they feel challenged. If you have a new boss, let them make their mark on the trees. Keep an open mind, support them in public as well as in private, and point out the occasional electrified fence, which is pretty much anything that will result in a very uncomfortable shock, like a higher-up's pet project. If you see the new boss going to hike on that, stop them first and explain why they may want to steer clear. Usually, they will be appreciative. If not, it can actually benefit you because, after the shock has worn off (pardon the pun), they will realize you have their back and are looking out for them.

Managing friends and former peers

As you rise through the ranks inevitably you will find yourself managing people who used to work alongside you. This can create problems for you, such as:

- Your friends' resentment of your success
- Expectations of preferential treatment (that's what friends are for, right?)
- They may think that they can talk to you the same way as before – wha'z up boyeee! Ok, maybe not...
- They may think that they can camp in your workspace and shoot the bull
- They may not understand that you cannot go to lunch and simply ignore Sally who sits on the other side of the wall and also is part of the team
- Etc.

So how do you handle this? The answer is simple and straightforward, but also excruciatingly difficult. You communicate with your new subordinates – all of your new subordinates, quickly. Sit down with your former peers and explain that while the only thing that has changed is your position, you still have to be careful that you are not perceived as showing any kind of favoritism. Do this as soon as possible, otherwise, your friends will create their own assumptions, and then talk with those that weren't your peers. Let them know that you are excited to be in the position and that you want to be sure that you are building a coherent team. Tell them that you are always available should they have any concerns and that you intend to build their trust with your actions.

The purpose of this exercise is not to remain on anyone's Christmas card list, but to ensure that your team has got your backend that you have theirs. Nothing can derail a manager faster than the perception of favoritism.

Beware of Management by Best Seller

There are a lot of very good business books out there with a lot of great ideas, which makes it tempting to finish a great book and go whole hog on what you just read.

Personally, I have worked with countless executives who have engaged in what I call Management by Best Seller, an acute condition where every time they picked up a new book, they devoured it and then proceeded to implement the strategies espoused within those pages. This would be fine if they didn't do it every time they picked up a new book with different ideas... One example entailed a Vice President who insisted on having the entire Human Resources suite repainted because she had read that a certain shade of blue had a calming effect. Once the proposal made its way to the CFO's desk, however, as you might imagine, the proposal did not have the same calming effect on the CFO.

Aside from being tiring, both for you and those who work for you, Management by Best Seller creates an environment of uncertainty, which can be detrimental to your leadership ability. A mark of a good leader is consistency your subordinates want to know that what they see on Monday will be the same thing that they see on Friday.

None of this means that you can't change how you approach things or implement suggestions you learn. All I am saying is that you do it incrementally. This increases the likelihood that the changes will stick, not only with your team but with you as well. Also, the changes will come as less of a shock to your people. On the flip side, if you are forever changing your way of doing things, the only consistency they will see is inconsistency.

So, if you do read a great book by the great management guru Jim Perkins, and you move into your organization to make the changes he advises, treat them like you would any other project:

- Plan it out,
- Mark milestones, and
- Have a vision for what you want the end result to be.

This is not to say that I am advising against making sweeping changes when necessary. There will be times when you need to make big changes, and you will need to make them quickly. When you find yourself at this point, keep a few things in mind and your odds of success will dramatically improve.

First, communicate the change to your peeps. Be upfront and direct. Tell them why you are doing it and how you see it affecting them. Tailor your message for each person, so that it is clear what you see affecting them specifically. For instance, if you have someone who is very ambitious and is regularly looking for ways to advance her career, look for ways that the change will open up opportunities or give them more exposure. If you have someone who is fearful of change, take some time to express to them that you know they are not comfortable with change, but you really need their buy-in. Regardless of the situation, if at all possible pick your associates up individually; it will not only help you tailor your message to them individually, but it also drives home the importance of the message. This is exemplified by the fact that you took the time to talk to them one-on-one. Additionally, by talking to them individually, you will have a better gauge on their acceptance of the message or initiative that you are rolling out. If someone doesn't buy in, you can begin dealing with those concerns early in. The bottom line is this: in all my years in Human Resources, I have never had to deal with an issue where a Manager over-communicated. That said, please do not misinterpret over-communication as talking a lot. Saying too much is a whole different ball of wax.

Second, ask yourself "when was the last time I announced a major strategic change/shift in my thinking?" If the answer is last month, then you should really give some serious thought to holding off for a while. If you change direction or course too often, you run the risk of losing your team when you do stumble onto a true game-changing idea or way of doing things. If you **do** decide to do an about-face on a recent initiative, eat some crow and tell your team that you recognize it didn't work and want to try something new. If you ignored your team's concerns and barreled forward anyway because you (thought) you knew best, apologize and ask for their support now.

Finally, set milestones to follow up on your progress and touch base with your team regularly to see how everyone is doing with the new initiative. Send out meeting invites for follow-ups over the next several months within minutes of making the announcement to let everyone know that this is something you are serious about.

So, here's the deal. Don't be afraid to make changes, even big changes; just be strategic about them and think them through before you go and make a fool out of yourself. It is common water-cooler fodder to talk about "strategic initiatives and changes" and how they change with the wind. With a little planning, you can avoid falling into this trap.

Putting the "No" in Nosey

Let's face it. As a race, humans are nosey. We can't help it, it's just how God made us. There is something in our genetic wiring that gives us an insatiable desire to be in the know. As a supervisor, this can be a real challenge because those that have been placed in your charge have the same desire as the rest of us, and while the line "that's on a need to know basis, and you don't need to know," might sound a little harsh, I'm not convinced that it's that bad of an approach.

As a supervisor, you are going to come into information that is confidential, sensitive, or proprietary, and you will be judged on your ability to keep your mouth shut. In the real world, knowledge is often seen as organizational currency and your people will want to collect as much of it as they can. By the same token, knowledge that is not shared is like money under the mattress – it is pretty useless until you use it. Further, just like idle money, it will burn a hole in the possessor's pocket, meaning they will HAVE to tell someone. If you think your people will keep a secret, you are absolutely wrong. And the more people they talk to, the more likely it is going to get back to someone who can have an adverse impact on your career.

So how do you deal with this? Simple, you tell them to buzz off. Ok, maybe not in those exact words, but that is the message you have to convey. How to go about it is up to you and your style:

1. If you are a straight shooter, something like: "I'm sorry, but that simply isn't something I can talk about," will probably work just fine.
2. If you are more of a soft peddler, something like: "I would love to share this with you, but I am sworn to

secrecy," might work. You may start there and work up to "look, I simply can't tell you."

Regardless of how you get there, the end result has to be that you do not give out the information. We all want to be popular, I get that, and "confiding" in people is a quick and easy way to get there, but never underestimate their own agendas. Never forget that they are asking so that they can bank some confidential information and turn it around to benefit themselves. And never, ever forget that it only takes one time to ruin your reputation, or worse.

On the other hand, there are few things more valuable than being regarded as someone who can keep things private. In doing so, you will find your own information wallet getting fat, which will likely lead to your real wallet getting fat as well.

All knowing does not lead to career growing

I once heard someone once say that you should never schedule yourself for more than 3 meetings in a day, otherwise you will get nothing done. The advice was given from the sheer fact that 3 meetings, at 1 hour each, means 3 hours of your day is gone, and that is assuming that don't go over and stick to their stated agendas, which is wishful thinking for a lot of organizations.

Another interesting thing about meetings is that nobody will admit that they like going to them, though there are people who do in fact like them. Those people who enjoy meetings typically fall into either one of two categories:

1. Those who like to hear themselves talk, and/or
2. Those who want to be in the know.

Regarding the first group, I don't really have any advice there, other than look in the mirror and recognize what you are doing and how this cannot be helpful for you. This type of behavior will be seen as a sign of insecurity and weakness, and the only way to combat this is through self-awareness.

Regarding the second group, it is a natural tendency for all of us to want to be in the know. It feels good when you are having dinner with friends and you are able to spout off statistics about your company. I mean, you must be important to have access to that much information, right? Either that or you have an internet connection and have heard of Google. The problem with being in the know is that it is not only very time consuming, but it is also often very annoying to your superiors.

Now imagine, if you will, the following scenario: You are the head of a project team in IT, and just left a meeting to discuss a new inventory tracking system that needs to be implemented. As soon as you get back to your cubicle, a very talented up and coming Analyst sits down and starts asking you about the meeting. Remember, you have just returned from the meeting and you need to formulate your game plan while it is still fresh on your mind and before you can even look at your notes there's Skippy sitting across from you, peppering you with questions. If you are like most leaders who have brought similar issues to me for help with, your first thought may be: "does this person not have enough to do?" Which is not a good impression to give off.

Now let's look at this through a different lens. Instead of the boss, you are a member of the project team. You are sitting at your desk when the boss comes back from a meeting and no sooner does she sit down but Skippy bounces up and starts peppering her with questions. Do you think more positively of Skippy now?

I am not saying that you should intentionally be kept in the dark and I am not implying that you should only work with information that is given to you. What I am saying is that you need to ask yourself if the information you are seeking is going to provide genuine benefit to you or the company, or are you are just looking to scratch an itch.

Put another way, ask yourself how often have you been completely satisfied with just a little bit of information. The answer is probably not very often. Do you know someone who is constantly up in your business? Does this improve your opinion of this person? Maybe they are even your best friend, is this something that you endear to them? Do you say to yourself "I love Jen, she is always asking me stuff that is none of her business"? So why do you think your boss is going to find this as a good trait in you?

Delegate your memory

Ah, priorities. We all have them, unfortunately, they don't always align with the priorities of other people. This is especially true if you are responsible for managing others. For example, one of my priorities might be to develop my team's overall goals for the coming year. In order to do this, it only makes sense that not only would I want to encompass what all the individual members of the team need to be working on as a unit, but also what they need to work in individually. Every piece is a part of the overall machine that is my team. One part of this machine is a project to develop a cleaner workflow for a system that one of my team members is a power user of, so it is a big piece of what I am going to evaluate her on. Now if I am going to be perfectly honest, I really don't care about the workflow issue. I never use the system and while others on my team do, it is not something that is really going to make a huge impact in the grand scheme of things.

So, is it beneficial?

Absolutely.

Does it need my support?

Definitely.

Is it a priority for me?

Not in the slightest.

In other words, this is not going to take front and center of my brain, so I will probably find myself forgetting about it. At least until my boss comes to me and asks how I am doing on the overall progress for my team.

So, what's a good manager like me to do? Do I tell them that their project isn't that important to me? I could, but I'm not going to expect anything for Bosses Day. The alternative is to inform them that I have a ton going on and that it may slip off my radar, so I need their help in remembering. In other words, I delegate my memory.

When you find yourself in this situation, it is imperative that you put the ball back in their court. Ask them to set up follow-up meetings with you, for instance. Remind them that it is their project and as such, they need to own it, which includes the necessary pieces that they need to get from you.

This technique does more than just help you remember, it keeps the project in the rightful hands of whoever owns it. The minute that they pass something along to you, they have washed their hands of it. The ball has left their court and is now firmly in yours. It is up to you now, and why not? You don't have anything else to do, you are the Manager/Supervisor/Director/Team Lead/etc.), so in their eyes, it's your job. When this happens, tell them that you will try and get to it by X date, but if they haven't heard from you, it is their responsibility to follow up. They should understand, and if they don't? You are the Manager/Supervisor/Director/Team Lead, so too bad.

One of the greatest challenge people have as they progress in their careers into leadership is getting out of the weeds. I have watched many a talented manager falter as they move up because they just couldn't let go of the minutiae. A lot has to do with letting go, but also, a good portion has to do with them not putting the ownership back on their team to follow up and holding them accountable when they don't come through.

It's lonely at the top

In closing, I want to leave you with one final thought.

Organizational structures are usually shaped like pyramids – in fact, many companies often refer to heads of divisions as "Pyramid Heads." So, it stands to reason that the higher you go in an organization, the fewer peers you will have, meaning it gets lonely the higher up you move.

This became evident to me very soon after taking on my first managerial assignment. I had some great employees, but I also had a few duds as well. In this scenario, one of the duds felt that he was more qualified for my position than I was. Moreover, he wasn't afraid to let it be known every chance he got.

One night, while talking to my Mom (I strongly recommend talking to your Mom every chance you get), this subject came up. After listening to me rant for a good while, she simply said, "well, it's lonely at the top."

It's lonely at the top.

That little phrase brought it all into focus for me. Why did I care what this guy was saying? I knew he was a mediocre performer at best and he certainly wasn't a threat to me or my position. As long as I was doing what the company needed of me, nothing else really mattered. I wasn't there to be his friend, I was there to get a job done. Incidentally, part of that was moving this dude up or out.

Since those days, I have seen more than a few managers fail to grasp this concept. The sad truth is that it is rarely a good idea to be friends with your employees, yet so often that is exactly what managers try to do. The sad truth is I have seen more than one promising manager brought to their knees because they wanted to be a cool boss; because they wanted to be liked. In fact, I have caught myself in that same situation on occasion, and I can tell you that in those cases it didn't end well.

If you are a manager, heed my advice and maintain a safe distance between those that you are supposed to be managing and yourself. This is not to say that you shouldn't go out to lunch, or the occasional after-work mixer, just don't get upset if you learn that they went somewhere and didn't invite you. If you want to be popular, or make friends, I would recommend taking a different, non-managerial career path.

Acknowledgements

As with any book, there is a lot of thanks to go around.

First off, this book would not even be a thought were it not for the never-ending support and encouragement of my wife, Kerri. Had it not been for her, I would have never had the courage to undertake this project in the first place. As with every other hair-brained idea I have had, she stood by me, and in this case read over my shoulder and provided invaluable advice and unending support.

Second is my dad. His fearless pursuit of his dreams was only hindered by his commitment to the well-being of his family. I will never stop looking up to him as the embodiment of someone who wasn't afraid to take risks and whose advise that "life's too short to do something you don't enjoy," will ring forever true. No one could ask for a better life-model than my dad and namesake.

Third, I have to acknowledge all the people I've worked with over the years for giving me the material that has come together here. Names have been changed because let's face it, some of y'all did some pretty stupid stuff and I don't want to get sued, but you know who you are (and in some cases so do the authorities).

Finally, I want to thank you, gentle reader. If you are reading this, you either skipped to the very end of the book to see how many pages there were, or you hung in there to the bitter end. Either way, you devoted some time to this endeavor, and for that I am grateful.

www.ingramcontent.com/pod-product-compliance
Lightning Source LLC
Chambersburg PA
CBHW050215230526
45470CB00001B/394